100% Career
SUCCESS

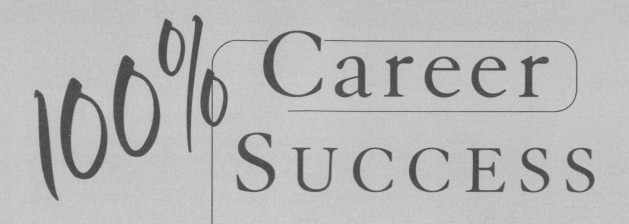

100% Career SUCCESS

AMY SOLOMON, MS, OTR

LORI TYLER, MS

TERRY TAYLOR, PhD

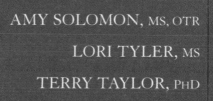

THOMSON

DELMAR LEARNING

Australia   Canada   Mexico   Singapore   Spain   United Kingdom   United States

THOMSON

DELMAR LEARNING

100% Career Success

Amy Solomon, MS, OTR • Lori Tyler, MS • Terry Taylor, PhD

Vice President, Career Education SBU:
Dawn Gerrain

Director of Learning Solutions:
Sherry Dickinson

Managing Editor:
Robert L. Serenka, Jr.

Acquisitions Editor:
Martine Edwards

Product Manager:
Jennifer Anderson

Editorial Assistant:
Falon Ferraro

Director of Production:
Wendy A. Troeger

Production Manager:
J.P. Henkel

Content Project Manager:
Amber Leith

Technology Project Manager:
Sandy Charette

Director of Marketing:
Wendy E. Mapstone

Channel Manager:
Gerard McAvey

Marketing Coordinator:
Jonathan Sheehan

Cover and Text Design:
Suzanne Nelson, essence of 7

Library of Congress Cataloging-in-Publication Data

Solomon, Amy, 1955–
  100% career success / Amy Solomon, Lori Tyler, Terry Taylor.
      p. cm.
   ISBN-13: 978-1-4180-1632-6
   ISBN-10: 1-4180-1632-2
   1. Career development. I. Tyler, Lori. II. Taylor, Terry, Ph.D.
III. Title.
   HF5381.S64617 2007
   650.1--dc22
                                                        2006019097

NOTICE TO THE READER

Contents

5   TIME MANAGEMENT 89

6   PROJECT MANAGEMENT 115

7 PROFESSIONALISM IN THE WORKPLACE 135

8 CAREER ADVANCEMENT STRATEGIES 161

Find It Fast

INFORMATIONAL SKILLS 69

Want to become more information literate?   See page 75

Need some suggestions for evaluating information?   See page 82

TIME MANAGEMENT 89

Want some steps for setting goals for effective time management?
See page 92

Need some ideas for getting organized?   See page 101

Want to learn some steps for building an effective schedule?
See page 102

Need some ideas for breaking the procrastination habit?
See page 107

Need some ideas for organizing e-mail?   See page 109

PROJECT MANAGEMENT 115

Want to know important steps in planning a project?
See page 119

Want some tips on scheduling project tasks?
See page 123

Need some tips on controlling your projects?   See page 126

Want to develop your skills as a project manager?   See page 128

PROFESSIONALISM IN THE WORKPLACE 135

Want to make a positive impression?   See page 139

Need some suggestions for keeping a positive attitude?
See pages 140–141

CAREER ADVANCEMENT STRATEGIES 161

Preface

CONGRATULATIONS!

If you are reading this book, chances are that you have completed or are close to completing your college education and are looking forward to entering your field. You are about to see the fruits of the efforts you have put into your education. Congratulations on reaching another significant milestone in your professional development!

THE ALL-IMPORTANT FIRST IMPRESSION

The first weeks and months of your new career are significant—the impression you make in your first job will have long-lasting effects on your professional relationships. The manner in which you organize your tasks, manage your time, relate to others, and manage personal issues that affect your attitude at work will lay the foundation for how you establish yourself in your new position. Demonstrating specific behaviors and assuming certain attitudes will help you make a positive entrance into your field. *100% Career Success* focuses on developing these workplace skills.

HOW WILL THIS TEXT HELP ME?

100% Career Success introduces you to concepts that, if applied consistently and conscientiously, can help you develop attributes that lead to professional success. Our approach emphasizes helping you learn and refine communication, self-management, and other "soft" skills that determine your place in your organization. This book's content is summarized by the following chapter synopses.

▶ **FINANCES AFTER GRADUATION:** Your finances change considerably after you graduate from college. Income tends to increase, but so do expenses. We address finances at the start of the text because leaving college with a sound understanding of financial issues provides a strong foundation for your financial future and for accomplishing other tasks.

▸ **LEGAL ISSUES IN THE WORKPLACE:** Knowing your rights and responsibilities in the workplace is critical to effective relationships and your performance. Understanding what constitutes discrimination and harassment, for example, helps you protect yourself and monitor your actions toward others. Workplace issues such as privacy and benefits are also discussed.

▸ **BUSINESS COMMUNICATION:** One of the most important professional skills is communication, both oral and written. The quality of your business correspondence with colleagues and customers represents you and your organization and speaks to your professionalism. *100% Career Success* provides you with a working knowledge of effective business communication practices.

▸ **INFORMATIONAL SKILLS:** The rapid rate at which information is disseminated today requires that you be able to locate, evaluate, and appropriately use data in a variety of formats and media. Using information effectively impacts your technical performance on the job as well as your ability to remain at the forefront of your field. This chapter helps you gain experience in obtaining and evaluating professional information and learn strategies for applying it to your professional growth and development.

▸ **TIME MANAGEMENT:** In addition to controlling daily tasks and meeting deadlines, time management refers to the manner in which you set and achieve goals. Day-to-day time management affects your professional credibility, and your ability to manage long-term goals contributes to your professional growth and career advancement. Chapter 5 addresses both daily and long-term time management.

▸ **PROJECT MANAGEMENT:** Project management is commonly thought of as a specialty in which trained individuals manage large-scale projects for corporations or organizations. The concepts of project management, however, can be applied to most professional tasks to maximize organization, keep projects on track, and evaluate results. You will learn the elements of project management and methods for applying them in Chapter 6.

▸ **PROFESSIONALISM IN THE WORKPLACE:** The impressions you make and the attitude you take in adverse situations contribute to how you are perceived as a professional (i.e., your professional image). How you address difficult relationships and resolve conflict in the workplace is also a significant part of your professionalism. Chapter 7 examines strategies for addressing difficult situations and people in the workplace.

▶ **CAREER ADVANCEMENT STRATEGIES:** As you become established in your field, you are likely to develop interests that will lead you to new levels of your career. Lifelong learning and continued professional development support this career advancement. Chapter 8 provides you with resources for your continued development and offers suggestions for enhancing you management and leadership skills.

HOW TO USE THIS BOOK

100% Career Success is written to help you actively develop skills that will contribute to your success and growth in the workplace. The following features will help guide you through the material and provide opportunities for you to practice what you have learned:

▶ **THE "BIG PICTURE:"** The "Big Picture" begins each chapter and provides an overview of chapter contents related to the other chapters in the text. As you read through the chapter material, you are encouraged to recognize and consider the relationships between the various concepts and information.

▶ **LEARNING OBJECTIVES:** Learning objectives provide a guide to the information in each chapter. Use them to identify important points and to understand what you are supposed to learn. Also, use learning objectives as a tool to determine what you have mastered and what you still need to work on. Remember, however, that the learning objectives are only a guide—you are encouraged to expand your knowledge according to your goals and interests.

▶ **TOPIC SCENARIOS:** Each chapter's topic scenario demonstrates the application of chapter concepts to the real world. Use the questions following each scenario to stimulate your critical thinking and analytical skills. Discuss the questions with classmates, think of your own application ideas, and raise additional questions.

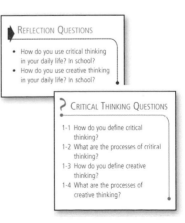

▶ **REFLECTION QUESTIONS:** Reflection questions help you to evaluate your personal development by increasing your self-awareness and your ability to understand your decisions and actions.

▶ **CRITICAL THINKING QUESTIONS:** Critical thinking questions challenge you to examine ideas and to thoughtfully apply concepts presented in the text. They encourage the development of thinking skills that are crucial to efficient performance in school and in the workplace.

Find It Fast

FINANCES AFTER GRADUATION. . . . .

Want to know what considerations are important when settin budget?   See page 10

Want some tips on managing your credit?   See page 14

LEGAL ISSUES IN THE WORKPLACE . . . .

LEARNING OBJECTIVES REVISITED

Review the learning objectives for this chapter and rate your level of achievement for each objective using the rating scale provided. For each objective on which you do not rate yourself as a 3, outline a plan of action that you will take to fully achieve the objective. Include a time frame for this plan.

1 = did not successfully achieve objective
2 = understand what is needed, but need more study or practice
3 = achieved learning objective thoroughly

	1	2	3
Define commonly used financial terms and principles.	☐	☐	☐
Discuss elements to consider when making major purchases such as insurance, houses, and vehicles.	☐	☐	☐
Explain how personal finances and credit are assessed and how the results of credit ratings can impact financial status.	☐	☐	☐
Describe steps for obtaining a credit report, criteria for reviewing it, and steps for making necessary corrections.	☐	☐	☐
Discuss considerations for financial planning for the future.	☐	☐	☐
Create a spending plan, based on net income and expenses.	☐	☐	☐
Discuss basic considerations of estate planning.	☐	☐	☐

Steps to Achieve Unmet Objectives

Steps	Due Date
1.	
2.	
3.	
4.	

▶ **APPLY IT!:** Following sections of the text, you will find learning activities that help you apply concepts discussed in the section to practical situations. Your instructor may assign these as part of the course requirements. If they are not formally assigned, we encourage you to complete them for your own development. *100% Career Success* includes the following types of activities, each indicated by its corresponding icon.

- **Individual Activities.** Individual activities are designed for your personal development.
- **Group Activities.** Group activities include projects that are more successfully completed through team effort and include several perspectives or broad research.
- **Internet Activities.** These activities are intended to help you develop online skills. For example, you may research a topic or participate in an online discussion thread.

You may find it helpful to combine the activity types. For example, an individual project may require Internet research. Some individual activities can be adapted to a group activity, and vice versa. Use the activities as guides and modify them in whatever way best supports your learning.

▶ **SUCCESS STEPS:** Success steps are included throughout the text and provide concise steps for achieving various goals. Success steps are offered as a summary of steps. Details of each step are discussed fully in the body of the text. Are you looking for success steps to achieve a specific goal? Use the ***Find It Fast*** table of contents to locate the steps you need.

▶ **LEARNING OBJECTIVES REVISITED:** Learning objectives are useful only if they have effectively guided you to learn and develop new skills and achieve full benefit from the chapter.

The Learning Objective Revisited Grid and instructions for its use are found at the end of each chapter. Revisiting the learning objectives provides an opportunity for you to assess the effectiveness of your learning and to set goals to expand your knowledge in a given area. An example of the Learning Objective Revisited Grid can be viewed.

▶ **SUGGESTIONS FOR THE PROFESSIONAL PORTFOLIO:** A portfolio is a collection of your work. A *learning portfolio* is used to track your progress through school, and a *professional portfolio* showcases your professional accomplishments. A *developmental portfolio* contains documents illustrating your professional development. A professional portfolio contains finished projects and other work that represents your best efforts and achievements. Throughout *100% Career Success,* we suggest completed activities to include in your portfolio; this collection can become the core of your professional portfolio. Arrange your portfolio in a way that illustrates your professional development and showcases your best work to help you review your progress and demonstrate your abilities. You may use your portfolio to document your developing professional interests and goals and the activities and projects that you complete to support them. Your portfolio may provide documentation for a promotion or other advancement.

SUPPLEMENTARY MATERIALS

In addition to the textbook, the following supplemental materials are available:

- ▶ **100% SUCCESS PORTFOLIO WORKBOOK:** This textbook supplement provides a format for creating your portfolio and expands the applications of the concepts presented in the text. Elements of the portfolio guide include additional explanations of textbook content, guidelines for journaling, additional professional development resources, and references to online activities. The workbook is an optional component of the *100% Success* series. If you or your instructor has opted to use the workbook, follow its guidelines for completing your portfolio.
- ▶ **THE ONLINE COMPANION:** Textbook and portfolio activities are supported by additional resources located in the Online Companion (OLC). OLC resources include additional activities, assessments, and suggestions for expanding your professional predevelopment beyond what is included in the textbook. Access the online companion at http://www.delmarlearning.com/companions
- ▶ **WEBTUTOR:** The WebTutor is an online course guide that complements *100% Success* series. WebTutor provides you with tools to organize course content and track your progress in the course, as well as a calendar for project planning. In addition, WebTutor provides links to helpful resources, access to discussion threads, and support documents, such as study sheets, and review quizzes.

BEYOND CAREER SUCCESS

After you settle into your new position, then what? As you develop new professional interests and goals, you will discover new directions in which to grow. Eventually, you probably will want to advance in your company and in your field. *100% Career Success* provides a foundation for starting on a positive and constructive note and becoming a successful employee. Build on this foundation by exploring and developing new technical and professional skills to increase your value as an employee and to support your career advancement.

A FINAL WORD

Look ahead. Keep your long-term career goals in mind as you read this text and complete its activities. Remember to maintain your professionalism and to demonstrate appropriate etiquette as you go about your daily work activities. Applying the concepts you learn from this book is the key—and the more you practice them, the more successful you will be in your new position. Again, congratulations on embarking on your career. May you have 100% success in your new position and well into the future.

Acknowledgments

The authors of the *100% Success* series would like to thank the staff at Thomson Delmar Learning for their tireless support and editorial suggestions. We also deeply appreciate our students, who have taught us so much over the years. Without them, this book would not have been possible.

We wish to recognize the educators and students who reviewed various components of *100% Success* throughout its development and contributed many thoughtful suggestions for the program.

Dr. Angela Alexander
Nicholls State University
Thibodaux, Louisiana

Douglas Allen
Catawba Valley Community
    College
Hickory, North Carolina

Kim R. Barnett-Johnson
Ivy Tech Community College
Fort Wayne, Indiana

Ashley King Brown
Catawba Valley Community
    College
Hickory, North Carolina

Katheleene L. Bryan
Daytona Beach Community
    College
Daytona Beach, Florida

Bettye A. Easley
Grant College, Suffolk
    Community College
Brentwood, New York

Marianne Fitzpatrick
Oregon Coast Community
    College
Newport, Oregon

W. T. Hatcher
Aiken Technical College
Aiken, South Carolina

Irene Gordon Jasmine
Nicholls State University
Thibodaux, Louisiana

Aleyenne S. Johnson-Jonas, M.A.
Brown Mackie College
San Diego, California

Debra M. Klein
Suffolk County Community
    College
Selden, New York

Sara L. Morgan
Minnesota School of
    Business–Plymouth Campus
Minneapolis, Minnesota

Kevin Pugh, M.S.Ed.
University of Colorado
    at Boulder
Boulder, Colorado

Susan R. Royce, M.S.
Design Institute of San Diego
San Diego, California

Leo Sevigny
Lyndon State College
Lyndonville, Vermont

Avette D. Ware
Suffolk County Community
    College
Selden, New York

CHAPTER OUTLINE

1 Finances after Graduation

THE BIG PICTURE

CHAPTER	
8	100%
7	87.5%
6	75%
5	62.5%
4	50%
3	37.5%
2	25%
1	12.5%

LEARNING OBJECTIVES

By the end of this chapter, you will achieve the following objectives:

- Define commonly used financial terms and principles.
- Discuss elements to consider when making major purchases such as insurance, houses, and vehicles.
- Explain how personal finances and credit are assessed and how the results of credit ratings can impact financial status.
- Describe steps for obtaining a credit report, criteria for reviewing it, and steps for making necessary corrections.
- Discuss considerations for financial planning for the future.
- Create a spending plan, based on net income and expenses.
- Discuss basic considerations of estate planning.

1

TOPIC SCENARIO

Brad has just graduated from college and has secured the position of his choice with a well-known software company. He will be earning a good starting salary for his field and for his geographic location. Brad is shopping for a new car, considering purchasing a home (or at least moving into an upscale apartment), and, in general, happily anticipating the financial freedom he was waiting for during his years as a student. Brad has student loans to repay, and he accrued some credit card debt while in school, but given his lucrative new position and salary, he is not concerned about these debts.

Based on this scenario, answer the following questions:

- ❱ Even though Brad will be making a good salary, what aspects of income would he be wise to consider?
- ❱ As a new graduate, what kids of expenses can Brad expect to incur?
- ❱ What additional expenses should Brad consider?
- ❱ What advice would you give to Brad about his "financial freedom"?
- ❱ What should Brad consider regarding his planned major purchases?
- ❱ What advice would you give Brad regarding financial planning for the future?

UNDERSTANDING FINANCES AND EXPENSES

In *CNN Money,* writer Pat Curry (2005) reports on a survey in which financial experts listed the most significant "financial surprises" faced by college graduates. Curry defined the following money-management topics as ones to consider to avoid being caught off guard by these "surprises."

UNDERSTANDING INCOME

One of the most important elements of financial planning is understanding the difference between gross and net income. Gross income is your income before taxes, insurance costs, and other deductions are taken out. Net income is your income after deductions are made from it—it is the amount you actually take home. Although employers quote the gross salary (amount before taxes) as your wages, the amount that you actually receive is less because federal, state, and local taxes and insurance costs are deducted from

1

the gross salary. As a result, it is important to plan your finances based on your net, versus your gross, income.

UNDERSTANDING TAXES

The amount of taxes deducted, or subtracted, from a paycheck can be surprising. Deductions represent adjustments that you can make to the amount of taxes withheld from your pay and are based on the number of individuals you are supporting. In general terms, more deductions mean that you increase cash flow coming in with your paychecks, but you may owe more taxes at the end of the year. You may have questions regarding the number of deductions you can claim, as well as about other expenses that can be deducted at year's end. Deductions must be planned ahead of time and documented accurately. Consider consulting a tax professional to help you plan for deductions and to help you understand your options within the parameters of the law.

UNDERSTANDING EXPENSES

It is sometimes a shock to new graduates to discover that, despite making more money, expenses can still seem overwhelming. Living expenses such as food, clothing, utilities, and leisure costs add up. In addition, standing monthly expenses such as rent or mortgage, car payments, repayment of student loans and other debts, and insurance premiums also are taken from net income. Having a family compounds these expenses. Realistically assess your expenses by listing them in a budget format and consider them in terms of your net income.

apply it

Cost of Living Calculators

STEP 1: Complete an Internet search using "cost of living calculators" as your search term.

STEP 2: Select a calculator and follow the directions provided.

STEP 3: Assess your results. Does the cost of living surprise you? How does the estimated cost of living compare with your net earnings?

STEP 4: Record your reactions in a journal format. Consider filing your recorded thoughts in the journal section of your Learning Portfolio.

Using the skills of a knowledgeable financial professional can help you planning your investments and other finances to maximize your financial potential.

INSURANCE COSTS

apply it

Insurance Terms and Questions

GOAL: *To understand terminology used frequently in the insurance industry.*

STEP 1: Skim the following section on types of insurance.

STEP 2: Record terms with which you are unfamiliar as well as questions you have regarding purchasing or using insurance.

STEP 3: Do the required research to answer your questions. For example, search for terms on the Internet or make an appointment with an insurance agent to explore insurance options.

There are numerous elements to consider when purchasing insurance. Graduating from college impacts many aspects of insurance eligibility and costs. Consider the following, based on Curry's (2005) findings.

▶ Students who have been covered under their parents' automobile and health insurance policies may no longer be eligible for the same coverage when they graduate. If you have been paying your own premiums during college, but have been on your parents' policy, it is likely that rates will increase significantly when you acquire your own policies (Curry, 2005).

▶ Automobile insurance rates may be increased based on the age of the car, who else drives it on a regular basis (which must be reported), age of the primary driver, size of the city in which you live, and, in some states, your credit history.

▶ Health insurance is another expense that sometimes catches new graduates by surprise. Many students have been covered under their parents' health policy, which lessens the cost considerably. Like automobile insurance, premiums can increase considerably when you are dropped from your parents' policy and assume your own policy. Curry (2005) suggests investigating COBRA as an option for extending parents' policies for a period following graduation, or extending your student plan, if that option is offered by your school. COBRA, which stands for the Consolidated Omnibus Budget Reconciliation Act of 1985, provides for qualified individuals, including dependent children, to maintain their health insurance coverage under a group plan (such as a family policy) for a designated time after they are no longer affiliated with the group.

1

Other students have had health insurance through their school, and the premiums for this insurance are also typically lower than those for other types of policies. Keep in mind that if an employer provides health insurance, you are likely to be responsible for paying part of the premium from your earnings (i.e., your share of the premium payment will be deducted from your paycheck). There may also be a waiting period before your employer's coverage goes into effect. Consider obtaining a supplemental policy based on the coverage available through your employer and based on your individual needs.

▶ Your home and belongings can be insured under a homeowner's or renter's policy. Homeowner's policies are typically required by the lender of your mortgage, and guidelines for obtaining homeowner's insurance are typically provided when a home is purchased. If you rent, rather than own, your home, it is wise to acquire renter's insurance. Insurance is something renters sometimes fail to think about, but it can be invaluable in the event of a disaster or accident. The landlord's insurance policy covers the building and property but does not cover tenants' personal belongings. Contact an insurance provider for more information on renter's insurance. Another insurance factor that can impact finances is whether your home/renter's coverage is for the cost of replacing the item (cost replacement) or whether the item is insured at its value at the time the policy is purchased. Think about this: Could a valuable belonging (for example, a stereo or camera) be replaced three years from now at today's prices? A cost replacement insurance policy replaces an item at its current cost.

▶ Disability insurance pays a percentage of your wages in the event you become ill or disabled and unable to work. Most employers offer an option for disability insurance. Like health insurance, it can be worthwhile to have additional coverage based on your needs.

▶ For all types of insurances, a deductible amount typically applies. The deductible is the amount you are expected to pay before your coverage picks up the expenses. For example, if your homeowner's policy has a $1000 deductible and you incur $2000 worth of damage on your home, you would be required to pay the first $1000. If the damage totaled $500, you would not be eligible for insurance coverage, based on your deductible. Deductible amounts can be per year, per incident, or per life of your policy. At times, filing an insurance claim is unwise if your costs do not exceed the deductible, as claims tend to increase premium costs in many cases. It is important to weigh the costs and benefits of filing an insurance claim. Consider the following illustrations using car insurance deductibles

1

as an example. As you read the example, consider the elements that you must think about when filing an insurance claim.

▶ **Example 1.** Bill had a car accident in which he incurred $3000 of damage to his vehicle. His insurance deductible is $750. Because of the laws in his state, Bill's insurance premiums (the amount Bill pays for his insurance) will not go up because he was not at fault. Bill decides to file a claim with his insurance and pay the $750 deductible, as this is the best financial decision.

▶ **Example 2.** Ellen's car sustained $1100 of damage when she backed into a light post. She must pay a $1000 deductible, and her agent informed her that her insurance premiums will increase by $250 on her next six-month payment if she files a claim. Ellen decides to pay for the repairs out of pocket, as this represents less of an expense than filing a claim and having her premiums increase.

▶ **Example 3.** Michael was out driving when he got caught in a hail storm. By the time he was able to pull into a covered garage to escape the storm, his car suffered $750 worth of damage. His insurance deductible was $1000. Michael was not eligible to submit a claim because the cost of repairs was less than his deductible.

MAJOR PURCHASES

Some major purchases, such as a home, can be considered a type of investment. In addition to calculating the monthly costs of these types of purchases against your net income, there are important considerations specific to the type of purchase you make. Homes and automobiles are relatively common purchases as well as major investments, so they are discussed here. Remember to research the same types of issues (such as financing, your rights, and so forth) when making other large-scale purchases.

Purchasing a Home

A home is one of the most significant purchases most people make in a lifetime. As such, there are strategies you can use to guide you through the process, as well as laws and regulations that protect you in this major venture. The United States Department of Housing and Urban Development (HUD, 2004) makes the following suggestions for purchasing a home.

▶ **Understand your rights.** By law, you are protected against unfair and unnecessary expenses, fraud, and discrimination. If you believe that you have been treated unfairly or dishonestly, or that you have experienced discrimination for any reason, you have the option of

1

contacting a HUD office for advice. HUD can also provide general information on your rights as a homebuyer.

▶ **Know what you can afford.** HUD (2004) indicates that most lenders follow the guidelines that a mortgage payment should total no more than 29% of the gross monthly income (this particular figure is calculated on the gross amount). Interest rates also affect how much house you can afford. Lower interest rates result in lower monthly payments, so it is important to seek the best interest rate. When you know your price range, you are better able to focus your search.

▶ **Know what you want.** Write a "wish list" that includes all the features you want in a home, noting those that are open for compromise. Like knowing what you can afford, knowing what you want also helps to focus your search.

▶ **Work with a professional.** Working with a real estate professional can help you through the intricacies of home buying. A professional knows the laws, understands the market, and is aware of loan options. The real estate professional's fees come from the seller, so as a home purchaser, you do not pay extra fees. Consider interviewing several professionals to find someone with whom you can work well.

▶ **Know your mortgage options.** There are numerous options for home mortgages, and it is your right to shop for and select one that fits your needs. The various types of loans each have their advantages and disadvantages, and the one best suited to your needs depends on your situation. HUD or your real estate professional can provide guidance in selecting the right loan for you.

Purchasing a Vehicle

Another major purchase most people make is a vehicle. Consumers have many options today, such as the choice of buying or leasing, and have access to a wealth of information via the Internet. The American Institute of Certified Public Accountants (AICPA, 2004a) suggests the following considerations when purchasing a vehicle.

▶ **Leasing versus purchasing.** Leasing an automobile may require less money initially but still incurs a monthly cost. In addition, there may be charges for extra miles driven or for "wear and tear" on the car. Be familiar with the terms of any lease and carefully weigh their advantages against those of purchasing a car. Remember also that when you purchase a car, it is yours when the payments are complete.

▶ **Shop around for a loan.** As with purchasing a home, numerous options exist for financing a vehicle. Banks, lending institutions,

1

and automobile manufacturers are examples of loan sources. Search for the best interest rate and other loan terms.

▶ **Understand the terms of the loan or lease.** Ask about terms such as the length of the loan, penalties (if any) for prepaying the loan or lease, and changes to monthly payments, such as a lump sum due at the beginning or end of the loan or lease. Clarify any information about which you are not certain. If purchasing a pre-owned vehicle, assess the loan terms to ensure that they are appropriate for a used vehicle. For example, you do not want a loan that will take longer to repay than the life expectancy of the car.

▶ **Know your rights.** Research state and local laws that pertain to vehicle purchases and leases. Many states and locales have laws that protect the consumer and give you recourse in the event that the vehicle you purchase or lease has problems.

▶ **Know your insurance requirements.** Know the insurance requirements mandated by state law, as well as by your lender. Your lender knows his or her requirements and can inform you of them. State requirements can be obtained from your state insurance commissioner's office. Aside from these requirements, consider the types of insurance that are appropriate for your car. Consider the amount of deductible you can afford, as a higher deductible can lower the cost of your premiums. Some insurance companies give discounts for various factors, such as a safe driving record or not smoking.

REFLECTION QUESTIONS

- What factors currently influence your finances?
- What changes can you expect as you become established in the professional world?
- What additional information do you need pertaining to insurance, making major purchases, and other aspects of income and expenses?

CRITICAL THINKING QUESTIONS

1–1. What do you need to do to be prepared for upcoming financial demands?
1–2. What resources do you need to develop an effective plan?
1–3. Where can you find these resources?

success steps

CONSIDERING INFLUENCES ON BUDGET

1. Base your budgeting on net, versus gross, income.

2. Clearly identify your expenses. Remember that even though a salary can seem lucrative compared to being on a student budget, expenses after graduation can add up.

3. Understand how taxes impact income. Be aware of deductions that you can take and understand how to document these throughout the year.

4. Be aware of your insurance needs and their costs, which can increase significantly upon graduation. Know what your employer offers in terms of insurance benefits and determine what you might need to supplement.

5. Know the process guidelines and be aware of your rights when making major purchases such as a home or vehicle.

apply it

Major Purchase Research

GOAL: To gain insight into the process of making a major purchase.

STEP 1: Select a "big-ticket item" that you might be interested in purchasing.

STEP 2: Research loan options, laws in your state that affect your consumer rights, and other elements related to the purchase.

STEP 3: Consider placing what you learn about making a major purchase in your Learning Portfolio.

ASSESSING YOUR FINANCES

Understanding your current financial status is critical to your well-being. The first step of any major financial activity, including financial planning and making major purchases, is understanding your credit report and ensuring its accuracy. Knowing your credit record and credit score and placing priority on maintaining a strong credit history is a crucial factor in successful financial planning and management.

THE CREDIT REPORT

A credit report is a document that summarizes your financial activity. It is available from credit reporting agencies, such as Equifax, Experian, or TransUnion, the three major agencies. A credit report includes your credit history for the past seven years and is reviewed by lenders when you request a loan for large purchases such as a home, or when you apply for credit (Quicken Loans, 2000–2005). The following items are included in a credit report and are the factors that determine your credit score.

Regular review of your credit report gives you the opportunity to find and correct errors on your record and helps you maintain a healthy credit history.

- **Payment history.** Payment history is the most significant item in the credit report. Payment history includes whether bills have been paid in a timely manner, whether any of your accounts are delinquent, and any history of bankruptcy or foreclosures.

- **Amount of money owed.** Quicken Loans (2000–2005) points out that owing money does not indicate a high-risk borrower or hurt your credit rating. Something that potential lenders consider, however, is whether you owe significant sums on several accounts, which may indicate that you are financially overextended.

1

▶ **Length of credit history.** A history of managing credit responsibly over time indicates a better credit risk than someone who has a shorter credit history.

▶ **Multiple new accounts.** A credit report shows when accounts are opened. Quicken Loans (2000–2005) points out that multiple accounts opened in a relatively short amount of time can indicate a higher credit risk.

▶ **Types of accounts.** Your credit report indicates to lenders what types of accounts you have, such as those with credit card companies, retail merchants, and home mortgages.

CREDIT SCORES

A credit score is a calculation that applies a formula to your credit history and statistically determines your level of risk. Many reports are generated by software made by a company called the Fair Isaac Corporation (FICO), so credit scores are also sometimes referred to as FICO scores (Wickell, 2005a). In a series of articles about maintaining a good credit rating, writer Janet Wickell points out that the three main credit agencies use different types of software to calculate FICO scores, which can result in different agencies generating different scores. So, you may want to obtain a credit report from more than one company or even all three companies.

The elements of a credit report are weighted to calculate your credit score (see Figure 1–1). Credit scores are assigned a numeric value from the low hundreds to more than 800, with higher scores representing correspondingly lower risk. Thus, a higher credit score can translate to more favorable interest rates and increased financing options (Wickell, 2005a).

Credit Report Element	Approximate Weighting in Credit Score
Payment History	35%
Amount of Money Owed	30%
Length of Credit History	15%
Types of Accounts	10%
Multiple New Accounts	10%

FIGURE 1–1. The elements of a credit report are weighted and calculated accordingly to determine your credit score. Each element is weighted approximately as indicated.

Adapted from Wickell [2005a].

1

CORRECTING CREDIT REPORTS

It is important to regularly obtain and review a copy of your credit report to ensure that the report does not contain errors. Consequently, it is equally important to keep accurate records of your finances. Wickell (2005b) suggests the following steps for disputing items erroneously included in your credit report.

1. Circle the erroneous item(s) on your credit report. Code each item so that it can be easily referenced in your explanation.

2. Write a letter to the agency explaining your reasons for disputing the item(s). Request that the agency investigate the situation. Send any documentation that you have that supports your claim. Mark each document with the code that corresponds to the item(s) code you have noted on the report. Send copies of the marked report and of any accompanying documents to the agency and save the original documents for your records.

3. Send your documents by certified mail, return receipt requested. In the event you need to show that you did indeed send the information, the mailing receipt is your record of proof.

4. Also inform your creditor of the dispute. If you do so in advance, the correction might be made before the creditor is contacted by the credit reporting agency, which is a routine part of an investigation.

Wickell (2005b) warns that credit reporting agencies sometimes are reluctant to change information on reports, in which case you are entitled to appeal the decision. If no change is made, you can request the credit reporting agency to insert in your report a brief explanation of the facts you have presented as part of your dispute.

Wickell (2005b) also indicates that it may be possible to request creditors to remove negative items, such as past due entries, from their records, provided you have kept the account current for a period of time. Remember that negative entries remain on credit reports for seven years, while items such as bankruptcies remain for 10 years.

RAISING YOUR CREDIT SCORE

If your credit score is less favorable than you would like, there are measures you can take to improve it over time. Wickell (2005c) makes the following suggestions.

▶ Pay bills on time, because late payments are a major factor in lowering credit scores.

Using credit wisely is an important step in managing finances.

▶ Keep your debt-to-available-credit ratio low by maintaining low balances on your credit cards or paying the balance each month.

▶ A zero balance on an unused account can help your credit score, so do not close an account simply because you are not using it.

▶ Avoid opening several accounts in a short period of time. Do not open additional accounts to improve your debt-to-credit ratio.

▶ Recognize that closed accounts can still be used in credit reports.

success steps

MANAGING YOUR CREDIT

1. Review your credit report regularly.

2. Understand what your credit score means and its impact on your financial activities.

3. Recognize erroneous information and take the recommended steps to correct it.

4. Take appropriate measures to raise your credit score if necessary.

REFLECTION QUESTION

• How diligent are you in checking your credit report?

? CRITICAL THINKING QUESTIONS

1–4. What items on your credit report require attention? What do you need to do to improve or correct these items?

1–5. If your credit report is strong, what has contributed to that? How will you keep it strong?

apply it

Obtaining a Credit Report

GOAL: To increase your understanding of the credit report.

STEP 1: Contact one of the major credit reporting agencies, such as Equifax or Experian. (You can research credit reporting agencies on the Internet.) Obtain a copy of your credit report.

STEP 2: Review the report for accuracy and to determine whether you need to improve your credit rating.

STEP 3: Make the desired changes to your credit score by setting goals regarding your spending or bringing accounts to current status as necessary. Follow up on any errors in the report.

STEP 4: Follow through with any adjustments that you make. Re-evaluate your report in six months and note any changes.

STEP 5: Consider placing what you learn about credit in general in your Learning Portfolio. Because this is highly personal information, you may wish to keep the more personal aspects in a separate file.

1

FINANCIAL PLANNING FOR THE FUTURE

Financial planning involves numerous considerations. In addition to managing spending and credit in accordance with net income, savings and investments play a major role in being prepared for the future. It is wise to consult a professional financial advisor who can assist you in meeting your individual needs. The following are basic investment concepts to consider.

SAVINGS VERSUS INVESTMENTS

Saving differs from investing. The Vanguard Group (1996–2005) defines savings as money set aside for short-term expenses, such as car repairs, and suggests that an amount equivalent to three-to-six months' worth of expenses be set aside in savings. Investments include money set aside over the long term to be used in the future. There are various types of savings plans and investment options to be considered.

SAVINGS PLANS

The Vanguard Group (1996–2005) suggests saving 15% of your income for short-term goals (i.e., goals that you wish to achieve within a few years). Certificates of deposit, money market funds, and other types of cash investments are recommended for short-term saving.

INVESTMENT PLANS

Investing over the long term requires careful consideration of your personal situation, including the blend of investments that best fit your needs, your assets and liabilities, your tolerance for risk in investments, and time horizons (AICPA, 2004a; The Vanguard Group, 1996–2005).

Investment Terms and Considerations

It is important to understand investment terminology and to consider the various factors involved in investing in order to ask your financial advisor effective questions and to understand the information he or she provides. Be sure to ask for clarification if a financial professional uses terms that you do not understand. The American Institute of Certified Public Accountants (AICPA, 2004c) suggests the following considerations when planning your investments.

> ▶ **Diversify your investments.** Diversifying your investments simply means dividing your investment dollars among several investment

1

types. If one investment does poorly, you still have others that are likely to be doing better. When the economy affects one type of investment, others are typically affected less. Your financial advisor can assist you in deciding on the best mix of investment types for your age, the economy, your investment objectives, and other relevant factors.

▶ **Select the appropriate financial advisor.** Some individuals are comfortable with their level of investment knowledge and enjoy the process of deciding on and managing their own investments. Others prefer the assistance of a professional. AICPA (2004c) defines three types of financial advisors: stockbrokers, money managers, and financial planners. Stockbrokers generally work for a commission and demonstrate variability in skill level. Money managers are focused strictly on investment concerns and charge a fee based on the worth of the assets under their management. A financial planner is concerned with all aspects of financial planning, including such investments as retirement planning, estate planning, and others. A financial planner's services cover a broader spectrum than those of a stockbroker or money manager. For any professional that you are considering, check the individual's references and investigate his or her professional credentials before making a commitment to his or her services.

▶ **Consider time and compounding.** As your investment draws interest, the value of your investment increases and subsequently draws interest on the increased value. This process is known as compounding and, over time, adds significant value to your initial investment. For this reason, investments over extended time periods increase significantly in their value (AICPA, 2004b).

Types of Investments

There are many types of investments. The following list includes 20 investment types cataloged by Investopedia, Inc. (1999–2005) as being investments that "every investor should know." Depending on your circumstances, these are investments that your financial professional might recommend and that you might wish to research.

▶ American Depository Receipt (ADR)

▶ Annuity

▶ Closed-End Investment Fund

▶ Collectibles

- Common Stock
- Convertible Securities
- Corporate Bond
- Futures Contract
- Life Insurance
- Money Market Securities
- Mortgage-Backed Securities (MBS)
- Municipal Security (Munis)
- Mutual Fund
- Options
- Preferred Stock
- Real Estate and Property
- Real Estate Investment Trust (REIT)
- Treasuries (Government Securities)
- Unit Investment Trust (UIT)
- Zero Coupon Securities

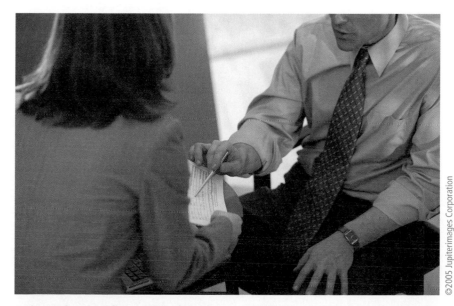

©2005 Jupiterimages Corporation

Understanding the different types of investments available to you will help you build a sound portfolio and spending plan.

success steps

PLANNING FOR THE FUTURE

1. Understand the importance of both saving and investing.
2. Strive for an appropriately diverse investment portfolio.
3. Select the best financial advisor for your needs.
4. Understand the concepts of compounding interest.
5. Select the types of investments that best serve your financial goals.

apply it

Investment Research

GOAL: *To develop an understanding of types of investments that may be appropriate for you.*

STEP 1: Conduct an Internet search using the name(s) of an investment of interest (see the list provided on pages 16 and 17).

STEP 2: Assemble information to help you learn about investment options.

STEP 3: Record any questions that you have and that you can ask of your financial advisor.

STEP 4: Consider placing the information you receive on investment options in your Learning Portfolio.

apply it

Financial Expert Guest Speaker

GOAL: *To develop a better understanding of financial investment options.*

STEP 1: Assemble a group of students interested in learning more about savings and investment options.

STEP 2: Assign one or two group members the task of locating and contacting a financial professional who is willing to speak or hold a question-and-answer session on investment options. Banks and investment firms may be resources for locating a speaker. Human resources departments may also be a source

1

of knowledgeable individuals, particularly in the area of employer-sponsored plans. You may also be able to locate existing seminars that are conducted by banks and financial planning firms.

STEP 3: Make arrangements for an expert or a panel of experts to discuss investment options in a presentation to students in your class or school. Ask students to prepare questions in advance of the presentation.

STEP 4: Consider placing the information you receive on investment options in your Learning Portfolio.

CREATING A SPENDING PLAN

A spending plan is a method of money management that allows you to monitor your earnings and make the wisest use of your income. It allows you to see where money is going and to determine which areas need attention, and it also gives you the flexibility to put resources where they are most needed (*Young Money*, n.d.). If you read the first textbook in the Delmar *100% Student Success* series, you may recall that a spending plan was also discussed in that text. Here, you are being asked to revisit that information, but as a professional rather than as a student. The process is the same, but your circumstances are different. The editors of *Young Money* (n.d.) magazine suggest the following steps for developing a spending plan.

1. Know your income and expenses. Keep your receipts and statements for several months to determine your average monthly expenditures. Calculate your monthly income by dividing your net annual income by 12. This provides an average income-to- expense ratio.

2. Categorize your expenditures. General expense categories and approximate percentages of income that are recommended to be allotted to each are as follows as suggested by *Young Money*:

   Housing: 23–33%
   Life/Car Insurance: 4–6%
   Food: 12–20%
   Charities: 5–10%
   Transportation: 7–10%
   Personal Debt Repayment: 8–18%
   Entertainment/Recreation: 4–6%
   Clothing: 4–7%
   Savings: 5–10%
   Medical: 3–5%

1

3. Keep records of your spending. Compare your actual spending to the amounts you have set for each category.

4. Make adjustments and changes as needed. For example, if you have extra medical expenses one month, you may spend more in that category and less in another. The goal of the plan is to allow flexibility while keeping you within budget.

---

success steps

CREATING A SPENDING PLAN

1. Assess your spending patterns relative to your net income.
2. Determine your expenditures and allot the recommended amount of your earnings to each.
3. Monitor your spending and determine how close you are to the suggested amounts for each category.
4. Adjust as necessary, staying within your budget.

---

apply it

Creating a Spending Plan

GOAL: *To develop a realistic spending plan.*

STEP 1: Follow the steps of creating a spending plan as outlined in this chapter.

STEP 2: Consider placing your insights into developing a spending plan in your Learning Portfolio.

ESTATE PLANNING

Estate planning is the process of arranging how your assets will be distributed at the time of your death (Legal Information Institute, Cornell University, n.d.). Like other areas of financial planning, estate planning is a highly individualized process based on your needs and wishes. You should consult a legal or financial professional to arrange the specifics of your estate planning. The following general considerations are adapted from The American Institute of Certified Public Accountants (AICPA, 2004d).

1

▶ **Take inventory of your assets.** Know what your assets are, including investments, cash, and insurances. Assemble the documentation of your assets in one place. In addition, you should have a letter of instruction, prepared with the assistance of your professional adviser, that indicates your plan.

▶ **Have a will.** The AICPA recommends that anyone of legal age have a will. Not having a will, called dying intestate, means that your assets will distributed by state law rather than according to your wishes, possibly denying your loved ones that which you intended for them as well as increasing the burden on them. A will also provides for guardianship of your minor children, management of your business and other interests in the future, and generally allows your final wishes to be honored.

▶ **Name an executor.** An executor is the individual you name to ensure that your wishes are carried out according to your will. The executor also has the responsibility of notifying appropriate agencies of your death, filing necessary paperwork, and completing other tasks to finalize debts and other concerns.

▶ **Consider advance medical directives.** Advance medical directives let your loved ones and attending medical staff know what medical intervention you desire in the event that you cannot speak for yourself. Medical power of attorney, for instance, designates a person to make medical decisions on your behalf if you are unable. These are aspects of estate planning that you should consider and decide upon with your family, in accordance with your belief systems, and while you are able to make sound decisions. Typically, these decisions are documented by a legal professional.

apply it

Estate Planning Guest Speaker

GOAL: To develop a better understanding of estate planning.

STEP 1: Assemble a group of students interested in learning more about estate planning. Assign one or two group members the task of locating a speaker.

STEP 2: Contact a legal or financial professional who is willing to speak or hold a question-and-answer session on estate planning.

continued

continued

STEP 3: Make arrangements for an expert or panel of experts to discuss estate planning in a presentation to students in your class or school. Ask students to prepare questions in advance of the presentation.

STEP 4: Consider placing the information you receive on estate planning in your Learning Portfolio.

CHAPTER SUMMARY

This chapter addressed multiple issues related to managing your finances after college. A major theme of the chapter was understanding financial obligations relative to income. Concepts such as considering net versus gross income, understanding the impact of taxes on your earnings, and the process of making major purchases were emphasized. You learned about the importance of credit scores, how to obtain and review your credit report, and how to correct report errors. Finally, you reviewed savings and types of investments and learned how to plan for your future with estate planning and advance directives.

POINTS TO KEEP IN MIND

In this chapter, several main points were discussed in detail:

- New graduates are often surprised by financial obligations following graduation.
- It is critical to consider all expenses in terms of net income.
- Purchasing insurance wisely includes considering elements such as deductibles, amount of coverage and need for supplemental policies, and other factors influencing the policy.
- Managing taxes requires advance planning for deductible items and accurate documentation.
- Your credit report provides a credit score, which significantly affects your financial status and ability to make major purchases.
- You can view your credit report and should address any errors as well as take measures to raise your credit score.
- Financial planning for the future includes both saving for short-term goals and investing for long-term goals.
- You and your financial advisor can select from a variety of investment options based on your individual needs and goals.

1

▶ Creating a spending plan based on net income and expenses allows you flexibility within your means.

▶ Estate planning with a qualified professional is critical to seeing that your assets are disbursed at your death according to your wishes and that other concerns, such as the care of children, occur according to your directions.

▶ Advance medical directives inform attending medical staff and loved ones of the medical care you desire in the event that you are unable to speak for yourself.

LEARNING OBJECTIVES REVISITED

Review the learning objectives for this chapter and rate your level of achievement for each objective using the rating scale provided. For each objective on which you do not rate yourself as a 3, outline a plan of action that you will take to fully achieve the objective. Include a time frame for this plan.

1 = did not successfully achieve objective
2 = understand what is needed, but need more study or practice
3 = achieved learning objective thoroughly

	1	2	3
Define commonly used financial terms and principles.	☐	☐	☐
Discuss elements to consider when making major purchases such as insurance, houses, and vehicles.	☐	☐	☐
Explain how personal finances and credit are assessed and how the results of credit ratings can impact financial status.	☐	☐	☐
Describe steps for obtaining a credit report, criteria for reviewing it, and steps for making necessary corrections.	☐	☐	☐
Discuss considerations for financial planning for the future.	☐	☐	☐
Create a spending plan, based on net income and expenses.	☐	☐	☐
Discuss basic considerations of estate planning.	☐	☐	☐

Steps to Achieve Unmet Objectives

Steps   Due Date

1. _____   _____

2. _____   _____

3. _____   _____

4. _____   _____

1

SUGGESTED ITEMS FOR LEARNING PORTFOLIO

Refer to the "Developing Portfolios" section at the front of this textbook for more information on learning portfolios.

- Reflection Questions and Answers
- Obtaining a Credit Report (Include information that you feel is appropriate): This activity is designed to help you understand your credit report.
- Major Purchase Research: This activity will provide you with insight into making a major purchase such as a home or vehicle.
- Financial Expert Guest Speaker: This activity is designed to provide you with investment information from a financial professional.
- Investment Research: This activity will help you understand different types of investments.
- Creating a Spending Plan: The goal of this activity is to help you understand your expenses relative to your income.
- Estate Planning Guest Speaker: The purpose of this activity is to provide estate planning information from a professional in the field.

REFERENCES

The American Institute of Public Accountants. (2004a). Personal financial planning [electronic version]. Retrieved March 4, 2005, from http://pfp.aicpa.org/Resources/Consumer+Content/ Learn+More+About+Personal+Financial+Planning/

The American Institute of Public Accountants. (2004b). Investment planning—the basics [electronic version]. Retrieved March 4, 2005, from http://www.360financialliteracy.org/Financial+Topics/ Investmet+Planning/Articles/Investment+planning—the+basics.htm

The American Institute of Public Accountants. (2004c). Creating an investment portfolio [electronic version]. Retrieved May 3, 2005, from http://www.360financialliteracy.org/Financial+Topics/ Investmet+Planning/Articles/Choosing+investments+vehicle/ Creating+an+investment+portfolio.htm

The American Institute of Public Accountants. (2004d). Estate planning: Protecting your family, providing for your wishes [electronic version]. Retrieved March 4, 2005, from http://pfp.aicpa.org/Resources/

Consumer+Content/Learn+More+About+Personal+Financial+
Planning+Protecting+Your+Family+Providing+for+Your+Wishes.htm

Curry, P. (2005). Post-graduate finance [electronic version]. Cable News
Network, LP, LLLP: A Time-Warner Company. Retrieved May 2,
2005, from http://money.cnn.com/2000/10/26/banking/q_bankrate/

Investopedia, Inc. (1999–2005). Investments to know [electronic version].
Retrieved May 3, 2005, from http://www.investopedia.com/
university/20_investments/

The Legal Information Institute. (n.d.). Estate planning: An overview
[electronic version]. "Law about . . ." pages, Cornell University.
Retrieved May 4, 2005, from http://www.law.cornell.edu/topics/
estate_planning.html

Quicken Loans. (2000–2005). Understanding credit reports and scores
[electronic version]. Retrieved May 1, 2005, from http://www
.quickenloans.com/mortgage-news/article/50.html

The United States Department of Housing and Urban Development
(HUD). (2004). Buying a home [electronic version]. Retrieved May 3,
2005, from http://www.hud.gov/buying/index.cfm

The Vanguard Group. (1996–2005). Personal finance for recent college
graduates [electronic version]. The Mutual Fund Education Alliance.
Retrieved May 2, 2005, from http://www.mfea.com/GettingStarted/
ArticleArchive/Cildren/Vanguard06.08.asp

Wickell, J. (2005a). How your credit score is calculated [electronic
version]. About, Inc. Retrieved May 1, 2005, from http://
homebuying.about.com/cs/yourcreditrating/a/credit_score.htm

Wickell, J. (2005b). How to correct errors on a credit report [electronic
version]. About, Inc. Retrieved June 19, 2006, from http://
homebuying.about.com/cs/yourcreditrating/a/correct_errors.htm

Wickell, J. (2005c). How to improve your credit scores [electronic ver-
sion]. About, Inc. Retrieved June19, 2006, from http://homebuying
.about.com/cs/yourcreditrating/a/improve_score.htm

Young Money (n.d.). Putting a spending plan together [electronic version].
Retrieved February 25, 2005, from http://www.youngmoney.com/
money_management/budgeting/020809_06

CHAPTER OUTLINE

Legal and Ethical Issues in the Workplace: An Overview

Legal and Ethical Issues

Leaving a Job

2 Legal Issues in the Workplace

CHAPTER

8 — 100%

7 — 87.5%

6 — 75%

5 — 62.5%

4 — 50%

3 — 37.5%

2 — 25%

1 — 12.5%

THE BIG PICTURE

LEARNING OBJECTIVES

By the end of this chapter, you will achieve the following objectives:

▶ Understand what constitutes discrimination and harassment in the workplace and provide examples of sexual and racial harassment.

▶ List and explain various laws that protect individuals from discrimination and harassment.

▶ Discuss how an employee can determine if he or she has been discriminated against.

▶ Explain methods for reporting discrimination and harassment incidences in the workplace.

▶ Explain the importance of employees understanding their legal rights and obligations in the workplace.

▶ Discuss methods that employers use to minimize employee misuse of office computers.

▶ Describe the various types of monitoring systems available to employers to track employees' computer activities and general productivity.

▶ Explain employees' rights to privacy and laws that affect the right to privacy.

▶ Discuss the purpose of the law of employment-at-will and explain its advantages and disadvantages.

▶ Explain the benefits that employers are required and not required to offer employees.

2

TOPIC SCENARIO

Over the last five years, Darlene has been an employee at the local hospital. About two months ago, a new manager took over the department where Darlene works. Recently, Darlene has been feeling uncomfortable about some of the behavior directed at her by her boss. For example, once when he was looking over her shoulder, he leaned in and put his hands on her shoulders. He has also occasionally sent sexually suggestive jokes to Darlene via e-mail.

Based on this scenario, answer the following questions:

▶ Is Darlene justified in feeling uncomfortable?

▶ What does the law say about Darlene's predicament?

▶ What should Darlene do?

▶ Have you ever been confronted with this type of situation? If so, what did you do? Would you do anything differently if confronted with the same situation again?

LEGAL AND ETHICAL ISSUES IN THE WORKPLACE: AN OVERVIEW

Employers and employees face a variety of legal and ethical issues in the workplace. It is the employer's duty to understand his or her responsibilities to employees, and, in turn, employees must be fully aware of their rights and obligations. This chapter is meant to give an introduction to some of the various legal and ethical issues that employees may face. Due to the breadth of information on these topics and the variability in laws among states, individuals are encouraged become familiar with how these issues relate to specific circumstances. The information provided here is of a general nature, and specific issues of personal concern should be addressed with a legal professional. The information in this chapter is not intended to be legal advice.

LEGAL AND ETHICAL ISSUES

The issues discussed in this chapter concern the legal rights and ethical behavior of employers and employees. It is the responsibility of each individual to understand his or her rights as an employee. Employees who do not understand their rights and obligations may not only be forfeiting rights guaranteed by law, but at the same time may be putting themselves in situations

▶ REFLECTION QUESTIONS

• With what legal and/or ethical workplace issues are you familiar?

• What legal and/or ethical issue(s) in the workplace concerns you? How might you address your concerns?

? CRITICAL THINKING QUESTION

2–1. If an employee's rights have been violated, what steps should the individual take to address the situation?

that may have serious legal consequences. Ignorance is not bliss when it comes to protecting yourself from potential problems with legal and ethical issues in the workplace. Arming yourself with knowledge is the way to begin protecting yourself legally and ensure that your rights have been honored. Be aware, however, that laws and rights vary according to state laws and the size of the company.

PRIVACY ISSUES IN THE WORKPLACE

Technology and the advanced use of the Internet have created a variety of both legal and ethical issues in the workplace. One of the most significant issues that employers have faced is the right of the employer versus the employee regarding the use of the Internet. Business lawyer Mark Grossman (1998–2006) highlights some of the issues that employers face regarding the use of the Internet in the workplace and affecting the need for Internet use policies. Grossman's findings include the following:

> The Internet gives employees access to sites and activities not related to business. Personal use of the Internet on company time costs the business.

> Cookies that are placed on a hard drive, such as those from adult Web sites, can be used against employers in certain lawsuits.

> E-mails can also be used as evidence against employers.

> Unauthorized use of copyright material (such as a graphic on a screensaver) may be considered copyright infringement for which a company can be held liable.

Using workplace technology for reasons other than work-related tasks is an ethical choice that employees must make. Many organizations have had to implement policies to ensure the appropriate use of company computers.

Grossman (2001) points out that the cost to business of employees surfing the Web during work hours exceeds one billion dollars annually. Although choosing not to abuse the Internet can be an ethical decision made by individual employees, many employees use the Internet for nonbusiness reasons during work nonetheless, and employers have had to take action in order to diminish the high cost of this misuse.

Many employers implement a published policy regarding use of office computers to try to curtail unauthorized use of the Internet in the workplace. Such policies stipulate that employees will use office computers only for company business. In order to enforce this type of policy, employers can employ a variety of monitoring options. The prevalence of these monitoring systems continues to be on the rise, according to a study performed by the American Management Association. Approximately 80% of employers use some type of monitoring system to track employees' use of the Internet and e-mail. Other systems include recording telephone conversations and video-taping (Towns, 2002).

2

An employer can more easily track an employee's computer activity and general productivity through the use of monitoring systems. The following list provides examples of monitoring systems currently utilized in business. These systems are examples of the types of information employers are capable of scrutinizing (Towns, 2002; Weil, 2000).

▶ A software product by WinWhatWhere Corporation is capable of tracking everything an individual does on a computer, such as opening windows, sending e-mail, and posting responses on discussion boards. The software sends a report to the individual responsible for tracking the activity. The software is undetectable to the employee.

▶ A monitoring program created by SpectorSoft Corporation takes randomly timed pictures of the employee's computer screen The employer can review the records at a later time.

▶ Software produced by Content Technologies called Pornsweeper is capable of reviewing images and tags anything that appears to be pornographic.

▶ Technology called "keystroke monitoring" allows an employer to determine what an employee types by tracking each keystroke. The technology tracks both saved and unsaved work.

apply it

Monitoring Systems

GOAL: *To gain understanding regarding monitoring systems.*

STEP 1: Schedule an appointment with an employer that uses a monitoring system.

STEP 2: Interview the employer and ask questions such as: What is the purpose of the monitoring system? Why was this particular type of system selected? Has the system been effective? What problems, if any, have occurred as a result of using the system? Write a short report regarding your findings and be prepared to share it with the class.

STEP 3: Consider placing your report on monitoring systems in your Learning Portfolio.

The increased use of monitoring equipment by employers has raised the issue of employees' rights to privacy. In general, the law has favored the employer as long as the employer clearly informs the employee of the existence of any monitoring systems and has published behavior expectations for office computer use and general conduct. Office policies regarding the Internet usually address the use of e-mail in the work setting. A standard policy commonly states that because the computer is owned by the employer, the employer has the right to know how it is being used and that employees should not expect privacy (Weil, 2000). As an employee, it is your responsibility to know your employer's policy. If one is not offered at the time of hiring, ask about it.

It is important to know your company's policy regarding personal phone calls. Court rulings have determined that employers have the right to monitor phone conversations if monitoring is done in the interest of business-related matters.

Privacy related to phone monitoring or recording has also received attention. The courts have stated that the employer may monitor employee telephone conversations if it is done to "evaluate business-related matters such as efficiency, productivity, and client service" (Towns, 2002, p. 5). It is illegal for an employer to monitor an employee's phone calls "if the employer knows that the call is a private call and is made with the expectation of privacy" (*Workplace Fairness,* 2005a, p. 1). Be aware that if your employer has published a policy that prohibits personal calls, the employer has a right to terminate the employee for violation of the rules (*Workplace Fairness,* 2005a).

As an employee, it is important to recognize that the issue of right to privacy extends beyond the workplace. Courts have determined that an employer has the right to know employees' personal information that affects the employee's ability to perform work-related responsibilities (Canter,

2

2005). For example, employers can complete credit checks on potential employees to determine their fiscal responsibility. Certain fields, such as those related to child care and the health professions, may require criminal background checks. It is critical to realize that what you do in your personal life can ultimately affect you as an employee.

EMPLOYMENT-AT-WILL

Private sector employees fall under the law of employment-at-will. The employment-at-will law provides flexibility to employers and employees to terminate employment. This law enables employers to release employees from employment at any time without providing any explanation or notice as long as the reason is not illegal (*Workplace Fairness*, 2005b). Employees have the same right to terminate their employment at any time. The disadvantage of this law is that as long as the action is based on legal reasons, employees do not have much protection from unfair treatment or being released from employment. For instance, according to employment-at-will, an employer can legally fire you simply because he does not like you, because he wants to hire a friend in your place, or because he has expectations that are impossible to meet. These reasons are ethically questionable, but they are not illegal. Currently, only individuals who work in Montana, Puerto Rico, and the Virgin Islands are protected from being terminated for unjust treatment. Union employees, government employees, independent contractors, and temporary employees are not affected by the employment-at-will law (*Workplace Fairness,* 2005b).

EMPLOYEE PHYSICAL AND DRUG TESTING

Depending on the type of work an individual will be performing, a physical exam may be required prior to employment. This is particularly true for health care workers or for those who will be performing demanding physical tasks. Documentation of immunizations or other health-related issues also may be required.

Other legal requirements of employment may include taking a drug test. This is particularly true for federal government employees. Drug tests may be performed on a random basis following initial employment. Employees must be notified in writing at the time of employment that these random and unannounced tests may be performed.

Pre-employment drug tests screen for numerous substances including, but not limited to, THC (marijuana), alcohol, cocaine, barbiturates, amphetamines, and steroids. Drugs remain stored in the body for varying periods following their ingestion. For example, THC can remain in the body for up to a month following its use. The amount of time that a drug

©2005 Jupiterimages Corporation

A physical exam may be required for some jobs.

remains detectable in the body depends on numerous factors, such as the drug's half-life, your metabolism, your body size, the method of ingestion, and the duration of use (CollegeGrad.com, 2005).

It is important to realize that certain prescription and over-the-counter medications can cause falsely positive results on drug tests. Usually, test-givers ask whether you are taking any medications. To be safe, you should list all medications that you have taken during the preceding month. If a false-positive result does occur, discuss the issue with the employer, explaining why you believe the result to be false, and request that a second test be completed. If your request for a second test is declined, you may wish to seek legal advice.

EMPLOYMENT BENEFITS

A variety of benefits may be offered to employees as part of an employment package. State laws and a company's size define which benefits a company is required to provide to employees. Benefits that are generally not required by law include vacation pay and meal and rest breaks. Benefits that are typically required by law include those pertaining to pregnancy and sick leave.

Although some benefits are not required by law, employers must consider what is ethically right in addition to what is legally required. Most employers want to treat their employees with respect and fairness, but offering appropriate benefits that are not legally determined is an ethical choice rather than a legal obligation.

The following is a short list of benefits that employers may or may not be legally required to offer their employees (*Workplace Fairness,* 2005c; *Workplace Fairness,* 2005d; *Workplace Fairness,* 2005e).

▶ **Vacation pay.** Employers are not required to give vacation time, although most employers choose to offer vacation time in order to keep productivity high. Companies have found that if employees do not take some time off, the rate of "burnout" is high and morale is low. To receive vacation time, employees often must be with the company for a certain period. For example, vacation time is often accrued each month and then can be used after six months to a year of employment. Most companies try to schedule employee vacations so that productivity is not affected. Senior employees typically have first choice of vacation calendar days. Some employers also have a "use it or lose it" policy, meaning that employees must use their vacation days within a certain time frame (commonly, the calendar year) and cannot carry over accrued days to the next year. Although employers are not obligated to allow an employee to take his or her vacation days before losing them, most employers try to be as

2

There are numerous federal laws that prohibit discrimination the basis of race, religion, gender, and disability.

accommodating as possible. Depending on state requirements, accrued unused vacation must be paid back to employees who quit prior to the end of the year.

▶ **Meal and rest breaks.** Employers are not required by law to provide meal or rest breaks unless the workplace is unionized or state labor regulations stipulate otherwise. The Fair Labor Standards Act (FLSA) requires that employers pay their employees for hours worked and distinguishes between rest breaks and meal breaks. Rest periods typically are paid time, while meal breaks generally are not (*Workplace Fairness,* 2005d). The length of a rest or meal break is at the discretion of the employer. Employers are required to provide bathroom breaks, which are a health obligation rather than a privilege.

▶ **Leave.** Although sick leave is generally not a legal requirement, many employers offer this benefit either on a paid or unpaid basis. Various types of leaves may be requested, including leave for the birth or adoption of a child and caring for a seriously ill child, parent, or spouse. Employer requirements for granting leave are set forth by the Family and Medical Leave Act and the American with Disabilities Act.

WORKPLACE DISCRIMINATION

Various types of discrimination can occur in the workplace, and many laws exist to minimize the chances that discrimination will occur. The federal antidiscrimination laws protect employees who fall into various categories of "protected class" (*Workplace Fairness,* 2005f). Employees can be discriminated against for a variety of reasons, including age, disability, immigration status, language, marital status, sexual orientation, national origin, pregnancy, race, religion, and gender.

Various laws protect individuals from discrimination. Individuals are encouraged to become familiar with the federal and state laws that provide them with discrimination protection. The following is a list of some of the federal laws (*Workplace Fairness,* 2005g; *Workplace Fairness,* 2005h; *Workplace Fairness,* 2005i; *Workplace Fairness,* 2005j):

▶ Americans with Disabilities Act of 1990

▶ Title VII of the Civil Rights Act of 1964

▶ Pregnancy Discrimination Act of 1978

▶ Family and Medical Leave Act of 1993

▶ Age Discrimination in Employment Act

▶ Older Workers Benefit Protection Act of 1990

2

apply it

Discrimination Laws

GOAL: To gain an understanding of the various discrimination laws.

STEP 1: Divide the class into small groups.

STEP 2: Assign each group to study one or two laws that directly deal with discrimination. Each group should gain as much knowledge as possible regarding those laws and then present a brief report to the class.

STEP 3: Exchange copies of each group's work. File the information in your Learning Portfolio for future reference.

Proving discrimination requires that the employee fall into a protected class status and can show either direct or circumstantial evidence of the discrimination (*Workplace Fairness,* 2005f). The following are questions that may be asked to assist an employee in substantiating circumstantial evidence of the apparent discrimination (*Workplace Fairness,* 2005f, p. 2):

1. "Were you treated differently than a similarly situated person who is not in your protected class?"

2. "Did managers or supervisors regularly make rude or derogatory comments directed at your protected class status or at all members of your class and related to work?"

3. "Are the circumstances of your treatment so unusual, egregious, unjust, or severe as to suggest discrimination?"

4. "Does your employer have a history of showing bias toward persons in your protected class?"

5. "Are there noticeably few employees of your protected class at your workplace?"

6. "Have you noticed that other employees of your protected class seem to be singled out for adverse treatment or are put in dead-end jobs?"

7. "Have you heard other employees in your protected class complain about discrimination, particularly by the supervisor or manager who took the adverse action against you?"

8. "Are there statistics that show favoritism toward or bias against any group?"

9. "Did your employer violate well-established company policy in the way it treated you?"

10. "Did your employer retain less qualified, nonprotected employees in the same job?"

2

If an employee believes that discrimination has occurred, it is imperative to report the perceived discrimination to the appropriate authorities. Documenting the occurrence(s) is critical, so keep as complete a record of the incident(s) as possible, including time, date, and the names of any witnesses. For further advice, contact your state's Equal Employment Opportunity Commission. If the issue is related to family and medical leave discrimination, call the Department of Labor (*Workplace Fairness,* 2005h).

HARASSMENT IN THE WORKPLACE

Harassment at work can come in a variety of forms. The two most common forms are sexual and racial harassment. Any form of harassment is illegal and should not be tolerated in the workplace.

Sexual Harassment

As an employee, it is important to know when you may be experiencing sexual harassment on the job. Sexual harassment can be experienced by men and women, and it can occur between opposite-sex or same-sex individuals. State laws and Title VII of the Civil Rights Act of 1964 make it illegal for an individual to be sexually harassed in the workplace. The following are some examples of sexual harassment conduct (*Workplace Fairness,* 2005k, p. 3):

- **Verbal or written conduct.** Comments about clothing, personal behavior, or your body; sexual or sex-based jokes; requesting sexual favors or repeatedly asking you out; making sexual innuendoes, spreading rumors about your personal or sexual life; or threatening you
- **Physical conduct.** Rape or assault, impeding or blocking your movement, inappropriate touching of your body or clothing, kissing, hugging, patting, stroking
- **Nonverbal conduct.** Looking up and down your body, making derogatory gestures or facial expressions of a sexual nature, following or stalking you
- **Visual displays.** Posters, drawings, pictures, screensavers, or e-mails of a sexual nature

If an employee believes that he or she is experiencing sexual harassment, it is important to address the situation by taking the following steps (*Workplace Fairness,* 2005k):

> **Step 1.** Inform the harasser that you are not interested. For future legal actions, it is important that you establish from the very beginning that the behavior is not welcome. Be as direct as possible in saying "no."

Step 2. Document the incident(s). It will be helpful for you to be able to provide documentation at a later time. Record all the event(s), including both parties' behavior, the time, the date, and the names of any witness(es).

Step 3. If the harasser is not your direct supervisor, alert your supervisor, administrator, or personnel director of the situation. If the harasser is your direct supervisor, alerting the personnel director might be your best alternative. Provide the documentation as required. If the harasser is your supervisor and no other individual is available, report the problem to legal counsel.

Step 4. Communicate with other coworkers, family members, and friends about the incident(s). This is important not only to gain support, but it may be necessary later as evidence regarding the problem.

Step 5. If the sexual harassment continues, even after the employer's involvement, seek legal advice from an attorney or the Equal Employment Opportunity Commission.

---

success steps

STEPS FOR ADDRESSING HARASSMENT IN THE WORKPLACE

1. Inform the harasser that you are not interested.

2. Documents the incident(s).

3. If the harasser is not your direct supervisor, alert your supervisor, administrator, or personnel director of the situation. If the harasser is your direct supervisor, alerting the personnel director might be your best alternative.

4. Communicate to others regarding the incident.

5. If the harassment continues after the employer's involvement, legal counsel may be appropriate.

Racial Harassment

"Racial harassment is unwelcome behavior that happens to you because of your race, such as verbal or physical conduct of a racial nature" (*Workplace Fairness,* 2005l, p. 1). Although no specific federal and state laws make race-based harassment illegal, racial harassment is considered to be a form of race discrimination and, as such, is covered under Title VII of the Civil Rights Act of 1964 (*Workplace Fairness,* 2005l). Forms of racial harassment are very similar to those described earlier for sexual harassment. The difference is that the individual is experiencing harassment based on their race versus gender

Leaving your job for new employment opportunities requires obtaining references from and closure with your current employer.

©Digital Vision

or sexuality. As with sexual harassment, reporting race harassment is important. To report racial harassment, follow the same steps as for reporting sexual harassment.

LEAVING A JOB

Exiting a job occurs either voluntarily or involuntarily. If you are leaving voluntarily and on good terms, it is appropriate to give your employer at least a two-week notice. Most employers either have the employee stay for the final two weeks or let the employee leave immediately with pay for the two weeks. Complete the following tasks prior to leaving a job (*Workplace Fairness,* 2005m):

▶ Obtain letters of references.

▶ Negotiate a severance package if the situation warrants one.

▶ Establish that the company is willing to rehire you at a later date.

▶ Be aware of signed contracts with possible industry noncompete clauses. If you do not have a copy of your contract, obtain one prior to leaving the company. In the event any questions arise, for instance, regarding an issue such as a noncompete clause, having a copy of your contract will help you determine the legitimacy of the employer's claim.

Although no one wants to experience being fired, it does happen. If it does, it is important that you obtain in writing the reason you were terminated. Depending on the state in which you live, the employer might be legally obligated to provide such a written explanation. If your employer is not required by law to provide one, and you are unable to obtain one, get a verbal statement from your employer. Record the reason and the date, time, and place that the statement was made. Note the names of any witnesses. Read it back to your supervisor/employer, request confirmation, and note the date (*Workplace Fairness,* 2005m). If the termination is involuntary and the employee is in good standing, then the employee likely is eligible for unemployment compensation.

Regardless of whether termination is voluntary or involuntary, it is the employer's responsibility to deliver the employee's last paycheck within a reasonable time, usually within 30 days or on the next payday (*Workplace Fairness,* 2005n, p. 1).

It is important to be aware that after you have left a place of employment and begun the search for a new job, your previous employer has the legal right to comment on your abilities, performance, or attitude. The courts have determined that employers have a right to know information about an individual that is relevant to that individual's employment

▶ REFLECTION QUESTION

• What other legal and ethical workplace issues do you think are important for you to be familiar with?

? CRITICAL THINKING QUESTION

2–2. How would you respond to the following statement: "Laws change so much that it is impossible to stay current with all the laws that affect employment"?

(Spolter, 2005). This is why it is important to leave an employer on good terms to as great an extent as possible.

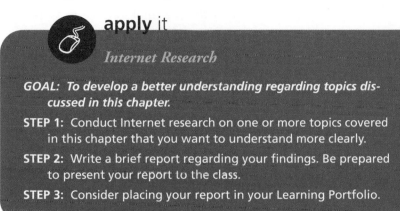

apply it

Internet Research

GOAL: *To develop a better understanding regarding topics discussed in this chapter.*

STEP 1: Conduct Internet research on one or more topics covered in this chapter that you want to understand more clearly.

STEP 2: Write a brief report regarding your findings. Be prepared to present your report to the class.

STEP 3: Consider placing your report in your Learning Portfolio.

CHAPTER SUMMARY

This chapter explored the rights and responsibilities of employers and employees in the workplace, as well as your rights to privacy and employers' rights to monitor employees' behavior. You were introduced to the laws that affect your rights as an employee and learned steps to take in the event you experience harassment or discrimination. You learned what benefits employers are legally required to provide and the factors that determine those benefits. Finally, you learned appropriate considerations for leaving a job and how to do so while maintaining positive professional relationships.

POINTS TO KEEP IN MIND

In this chapter, several main points were discussed in detail:

- It is the responsibility of both the employer and employee to understand their rights and obligations in the workplace.
- Many employers use monitoring systems to track employees' computer activities and general productivity.
- Laws regarding privacy favor the employer as long as the employer clearly informs the employee of the existence of monitoring systems and the expectations for office computer use.
- The purpose of the employment-at-will law is to allow employers and employees the flexibility of deciding when to terminate employment.
- The downside of the employment-at-will law is that as long as an employer does not engage in an illegal action, employees do not

2

have much protection from being released from employment and experiencing unfair treatment.

▶ There are no legal standard for treating employees fairly except in the state of Montana and in Puerto Rico and the Virgin Islands.

▶ Individual state laws and company size affect what benefits a company must offer to its employees.

▶ Employers are not required to give their employees vacation time, although most employers choose to do so in order to keep productivity and morale high.

▶ Employers are not required by law to provide meal or rest breaks unless the workplace is unionized or state labor regulations indicate otherwise.

▶ Although sick leave is generally not a legally required benefit, many employers offer it either on a paid or unpaid basis.

▶ Discrimination in the workplace can occur for a variety of reasons, including age, disability, immigration status, language, marital status, sexual orientation, national origin, pregnancy, race, religion, and gender.

▶ Federal laws that protect individuals from discrimination include the Americans with Disabilities Act of 1990, Title VII of the Civil Rights Act of 1964, the Pregnancy Discrimination Act of 1978, the Family and Medical Leave Act of 1993, the Age Discrimination in Employment Act, and the Older Workers Benefit Protection Act of 1990.

▶ Any form of harassment is illegal and should not be tolerated in the workplace.

▶ State laws and Title VII of the Civil Rights Act of 1964 make it illegal for an individual to be sexually harassed in the workplace.

▶ Racial harassment is considered to be a form of race discrimination and so is covered under Title VII of the Civil Rights Act of 1964.

▶ Items that should be obtained prior to leaving an employer include letter of references, severance package, and copies of any signed contracts or agreements.

▶ If an involuntary termination has occurred through no fault of the employee's, then the employee is likely eligible for unemployment compensation.

▶ If possible, leave an employer on good terms and with no bridges burned.

LEARNING OBJECTIVES REVISITED

Review the learning objectives for this chapter and rate your level of achievement for each objective using the rating scale provided. For each objective on which you do not rate yourself as a 3, outline a plan of action that you will take to fully achieve the objective. Include a time frame for this plan.

1 = did not successfully achieve objective

2 = understand what is needed, but need more study or practice

3 = achieved learning objective thoroughly

	1	2	3
Understand what constitutes discrimination in the workplace.	☐	☐	☐
List and explain various laws that protect individuals from discrimination.	☐	☐	☐
Explain the importance for employees to understand their legal rights and obligations in the workplace.	☐	☐	☐
Discuss methods that employers use to diminish employee misuse of office computers.	☐	☐	☐
Describe the various types of monitoring systems available to employers to track employees' computer activities and general productivity.	☐	☐	☐
Explain the rights an employee has to privacy.	☐	☐	☐
Discuss the purpose of the law of employment-at-will and explain the pros and cons of this law.	☐	☐	☐
Explain the various benefits that employers are required and not required to offer employees.	☐	☐	☐
Discuss how an employee can determine if he or she has been discriminated against.	☐	☐	☐
Explain how employees report discrimination and harassment incidents.	☐	☐	☐
Provide examples of sexual and racial harassment.	☐	☐	☐

Steps to Achieve Unmet Objectives

Steps   Due Date

1. _____   _____

2. _____   _____

3. _____   _____

4. _____   _____

SUGGESTED ITEMS FOR LEARNING PORTFOLIO

Refer to the "Developing Portfolios" section at the front of this textbook for more information on learning portfolios.

- ▶ Monitoring Systems: The purpose of this activity is to increase your understanding of monitoring systems in the workplace.
- ▶ Discrimination Laws: The goal of this activity is to increase your understanding of discrimination laws.
- ▶ Internet Research: This activity provides the opportunity for you to explore topics that are of interest to you.

REFERENCES

Canter, J. (2005). Drawing the line on privacy at work [electronic version]. Wall Street Journal Executive Career Site: CareerJournal.com. Retrieved April 11, 2005, from http://www.careers.wsj.com/myc/legal/19990209-canter.html

CollegeGrad.com. (2005). Drug testing and other possible conditions of employment [electronic version]. Retrieved November 24, 2005, from http://www.CollegeGrad.com/jobsearch/24-2.shtml

Grossman, M. (1998–2006). Employees, the net, and trouble [electronic version]. Retrieved June 19, 2006, from http://www.ecomputerlaw.com/articles/show_article.php?article=2006_employees,_the_net,_and_trouble

Spolter, L. (2005). Are you a victim of workplace defamation? [electronic version]. The Wall Street Journal Executive Career Site: Career Journal.com. Retrieved April 8, 2005, from http://www.careerjournal.com/myc/legal/19990503-spolter.html

Towns, D. (2002). Legal issues involved in monitoring employees' Internet and e-mail usage [electronic version]. Retrieved April 8, 2005, from http://www.gigalaw.com/articles/2002-all/towns-2002-01-all.html

Weil, G. B. (2000). Company e-mail and Internet policies [electronic version]. Retrieved April 8, 2005, from http://www.gigalaw.com/articles/2000-all/gall-2000-01-all.html

Workplace Fairness. (2005a). General info: Invasion of privacy [electronic version]. Retrieved April 8, 2005, from http://www.workplacefairness.org/index.php?page=generalprivacy

Workplace Fairness. (2005b). Classifications [electronic version]. Retrieved April 8, 2005, from http://www.workplacefairness.org/index .php?page=classifications

Workplace Fairness. (2005c). Vacation pay [electronic version]. Retrieved April 8, 2005, from http://www.workplacefairness.org/index .php?page=vacationpay

Workplace Fairness. (2005d). Meal and rest breaks [electronic version]. Retrieved April 8, 2005, from http://www.workplacefairness.org/ index.php?page=breaks#5

Workplace Fairness. (2005e). Sick leave [electronic version]. Retrieved April 8, 2005, from http://www.workplacefairness.org/index .php?page=sickleave

Workplace Fairness. (2005f). Discrimination: General information [electronic version]. Retrieved April 8, 2005, from http://www .workplacefairness.org/index.php?page=generaldisc

Workplace Fairness. (2005g). Disability discrimination [electronic version]. Retrieved April 8, 2005, from http://www.workplacefairness.org/ index.php?page=disability

Workplace Fairness. (2005h). Pregnancy leave [electronic version]. Retrieved April 8, 2005, from http://www.workplacefairness.org/ index.php?page=pregnancyleave

Workplace Fairness. (2005i). Race discrimination [electronic version]. Retrieved April 8, 2005, from http://www.workplacefairness.org/ index.php?page=racedisc

Workplace Fairness. (2005j). Age discrimination [electronic version]. Retrieved April 8, 2005, from http://www.workplacefairness .org/index.php?page=age

Workplace Fairness. (2005k). Sexual harassment [electronic version]. Retrieved April 8, 2005, from http://www.workplacefairness .org/index.php?page=sex

Workplace Fairness. (2005l). Racial harassment [electronic version]. Retrieved April 8, 2005, from http://www.workplacefairness.org/ index.php?page=raceharassment

Workplace Fairness. (2005m). Leaving your job [electronic version]. Retrieved April 8, 2005, from http://www.workplacefairness.org/ index.php?page=leaving

Workplace Fairness. (2005n). Final pay [electronic version]. Retrieved April 8, 2005, from http://www.workplacefairness.org/index .php?page=finalpay

2

CHAPTER OUTLINE

3 Business Communication

LEARNING OBJECTIVES

8		100%
7		87.5%
6		75%
CHAPTER 5		62.5%
4		50%
3		**37.5%**
2		25%
1		12.5%

By the end of this chapter, you will achieve the following objectives:

▶ Define *communication* and explain when communication is considered successful.
▶ Discuss the characteristics of effective verbal communication.
▶ Describe the characteristics of effective listening.
▶ Explain methods to strengthen communication between employers and employees.
▶ Discuss how to establish and maintain positive relationships in the workplace.
▶ Explain how conflict can be resolved.
▶ Discuss how employee satisfaction is reflected in customer satisfaction.
▶ Compare and contrast effective and ineffective customer service.
▶ List and explain the steps of responding appropriately to criticism.
▶ List and explain the "Seven Cs" of effective business writing.
▶ Discuss the general format of a business letter.
▶ Explain the basic format of a memo.
▶ Discuss considerations to be made when using e-mail and composing e-mail in the workplace.

TOPIC SCENARIO

Jean started her new job three months ago and has had difficulty getting along with one of her coworkers ever since. Jean doesn't feel as though the problem is a result of anything specific that the coworker is doing, but rather that the trouble is the coworker's personality, which is generally irritating to her. Jean is unsure what to do, but she believes her work is being affected by this personality clash.

Based on this scenario, answer the following questions:

▶ Should Jean just learn to live with the situation or should she confront the coworker?

▶ If Jean is to confront the coworker, what should the expected outcome be?

▶ How should Jean confront the coworker if the problem is personality based?

▶ Can Jean change in order to make the situation more acceptable?

▶ Should Jean involve her manager?

COMMUNICATION: AN OVERVIEW

Verbal and nonverbal communication in the workplace occurs in many situations, including one-on-one discussions, group meetings, conference calls, e-mails, and written correspondence. Your satisfaction at work relies to a great extent on your ability to use excellent communication skills. Effective communication makes interactions with others more satisfying and often increases productivity.

According to Accel-Team (2005a, p. 2), "Communication is a two-way process in which people transmit (send) and receive ideas, information, opinions, or emotions. In the world of business, the aim should be to develop communication patterns between individuals and groups that are meaningful, direct, open, and honest." Given the importance of effective communication, how best can it be accomplished?

Communication is greatly impacted by an individual's verbal and nonverbal messages and is successful only if all parties involved clearly understand the message that has been conveyed. Waughfield (2002) states that effective communication results under the following conditions:

▶ The sender uses clear and well-understood words to convey the message.

©Digital Vision

The ability to communicate clearly and effectively with a variety of people is critical to workplace success.

▶ The receiver hears the message that the sender intends.

▶ Verbal and nonverbal messages are consistent with each other.

▶ The receiver is receptive to the message.

FACTORS OF EFFECTIVE COMMUNICATION

Listening is a critical factor to effective communication. The following are guidelines to more effective listening are defined by Accel-Team (2005b, p. 2):

▶ Make eye contact with the speaker.

▶ Question the speaker to clarify meanings.

▶ Show concern about the speaker's feelings.

▶ Occasionally repeat what you are hearing to confirm your understanding.

▶ Do not rush the speaker.

▶ Maintain poise and emotional control.

▶ Respond with a nod, smile, or frown.

▶ Pay close attention.

▶ Do not interrupt.

▶ Stay on the subject until the speaker finishes his or her thoughts.

Communication at work involves a variety of individuals, including coworkers, supervisors, and customers. The success of any business can be measured by employee and customer satisfaction, which is greatly influenced by positive interactions. The impact of satisfying communication between employer and employee is likely to be reflected in successful relationships with customers.

Successful employers work diligently to ensure that communication is effective with their employees. McNamara (1999) suggests using the following devices to build strong internal communication:

▶ Written status reports on current projects submitted from all employees to supervisors

▶ Monthly employee meetings

▶ Weekly or biweekly department meetings

▶ Monthly one-on-one meetings between supervisor and employees

Other forums may be appropriate and effective depending on your individual work setting. For example, individual work teams often hold regular meetings to track projects and communicate progress.

©Digital Vision

3

Getting along with others makes the workplace more pleasant and contributes to productivity.

GETTING ALONG WITH OTHERS

Getting along with others is important to your overall career success. Improving your daily interactions with others at work contributes to productive professional relationships and requires consistent use of effective communication skills. Observing the simple guidelines listed below supports strong relationships in the workplace.

▌ **Be a positive person.** Negative or moody people eventually drain the office environment of positive emotional energy.

▌ **Observe and listen to others.** By doing so, you can learn a lot about your supervisor's and your coworkers' likes and dislikes. Draw on this knowledge to establish positive relationships.

▌ **Avoid unprofessional behavior.** For example, silliness and poor manners may irritate coworkers and distract them from the task at hand. Be receptive to feedback from others and alter your behavior as needed.

▌ **Learn to avoid "pushing people's buttons."** Be aware of issues and behaviors to which your coworkers are sensitive. Consciously avoid subjects and actions that annoy or anger colleagues.

▌ **Avoid rushing to react to others' actions or words.** Think through your responses logically rather than reacting emotionally. Too often people are quick to anger and to pass judgment. Hastily expressing emotions eventually works against you.

▌ **Have a genuine and caring attitude.** Develop a genuine concern for your coworkers' well-being. Approach colleagues with a helpful and collaborative attitude. For example, offer assistance if it appears to be needed.

▌ **Help others feel good about themselves.** Recognize your colleagues' accomplishments. Always give credit to the deserving individual. Offer genuine words of encouragement and congratulations for a job well done.

success steps

BUILDING STRONG WORKPLACE RELATIONSHIPS

▌ Be a positive person.

▌ Observe and listen to others.

▌ Avoid unprofessional behavior.

▶ Learn to avoid "pushing people's buttons."

▶ Avoid rushing to react to other's actions or words.

▶ Have a genuine and caring attitude.

▶ Help others feel good about themselves.

CONFLICT RESOLUTION

Conflict in the workplace occurs for a variety of reasons and can adversely affect productivity if it is not resolved. Conflict is often due to a simple misunderstanding that can be quickly resolved through discussion. Conflicts that occur due to personality differences, however, can be more challenging to deal with.

There are a variety of ways that an employee can help to de-escalate a conflict. The following are suggestions for conflict de-escalation are offered by Anderson (2004):

Step 1. Consider what you are really trying to accomplish: What needs are you trying to fulfill? How important is making your point in the greater scheme of things? Is it worth damaging the working relationship you have established with the individual?

Step 2. Avoid considering the other individual as an adversary. Resentment creates more conflict.

Step 3. Remain objective. Do not let strong emotions cloud your judgment.

Step 4. Demonstrate effective listening skills and your ability to put your needs aside to hear what others are saying. Avoid interrupting others.

Step 5. Repeat to the other speaker what he or she has said to confirm that you are hearing and understanding his or her position.

Step 6. Avoid overpowering the situation. If you do, you are likely to escalate the negative conditions and antagonize the other party.

Step 7. Strive to be fair to all parties involved when proposing solutions and remain flexible to consider a variety of solutions.

Step 8. Recruit an uninvolved person as a mediator if necessary. A fair and neutral party may be helpful in resolving the conflict.

3

► REFLECTION QUESTIONS

- What feedback have you received regarding your communication abilities?
- In what areas could you improve those abilities?

? CRITICAL THINKING QUESTION

3–1. Can an individual get to a point where he or she is proficient as a communicator or is there always room for improvement? Explain your answer.

success steps

CONFLICT RESOLUTION STEPS

1. Know what you are trying to accomplish by resolving the conflict.
2. Maintain a positive relationship throughout the resolution process.
3. Remain objective and control emotional responses.
4. Use effective listening skills and avoid interrupting.
5. Repeat what you hear to confirm understanding.
6. Avoid attempting to overpower the situation.
7. Strive for fairness and compromise.
8. Use mediation as necessary.

©Digital Vision

Being able to use corrective feedback to problem solve and set goals is an important part of your professional development and long-term success.

HANDLING CORRECTIVE FEEDBACK

How you deal with corrective feedback (commonly known as constructive criticism) makes a significant statement regarding your desire to grow personally and professionally. While some individuals are threatened by criticism regardless of its intention, others learn how to accept criticism and to select the comments that are important to incorporate into their development. Learning how to hear corrective feedback and respond to it constructively is a useful skill. Study the following process for responding to criticism (Anderson, n.d.):

Step 1. Acknowledge the feedback verbally or nonverbally. For example, a nod of the head or saying, "Yes, I remember that situation" lets the speaker know that you are listening to what he or she is saying.

Step 2. Control your emotions. Do not assume that the individual giving the criticism has bad intentions. People are sometimes well intentioned even though their approach is not the best. Responding with anger prevents you from hearing something that may be important for your own growth and limits or eliminates your opportunity to present your perspective. If feelings of anger become apparent on the part of either party, pause or take a brief "timeout" to allow emotions to cool.

Step 3. Clarify the feedback and encourage discussion by requesting additional information. Really listen during this time. Do not allow personalities or feelings to get in the way of an important message. Focus on what you can learn from the feedback. Be aware of the speaker's feelings and motives for giving the feedback. By listening, you can learn a lot about the real purpose of the encounter.

Step 4. Find something on which you and speaker agree and call attention to this point of agreement. Use it as a starting point for discussion. Doing so often helps the person feel as if you are hearing the message that he or she is sending and de-escalates any emotions that have become charged during the interaction.

Step 5. Provide your perspective respectfully and tactfully. State what you agree with in the other party's feedback and offer a plan for what you will do in response to the criticism. It is important to apologize if an apology is appropriate. Then, state your perspective, identifying it as your viewpoint and pointing out which elements of the criticism you disagree with. Responding assertively and responsibly gains respect from the person giving the criticism.

Step 6. Incorporate the feedback into daily activities. Ultimately, what feedback you accept is your choice. You may not agree with the criticism; however, it is still your responsibility to apply it to performing according to the expectations of your position. Consider how you can use corrective feedback as a tool for your growth and development.

---

success steps

ACCEPTING CORRECTIVE FEEDBACK

1. Acknowledge that you have heard the feedback by nodding or verbally responding to it.

2. Control your emotions.

3. Ask for additional information. Remain focused on the issue. Avoid finding fault with an individual or personality.

4. Find common ground on which you and the other person agree. Use that point of agreement as a basis for discussion.

5. Provide your perspective of the situation respectfully and tactfully.

6. Incorporate the feedback into your daily activities.

REFLECTION QUESTIONS

- How do you handle criticism?
- When someone criticizes you, what is your natural reaction?
- How can you improve how you handle criticism?

CRITICAL THINKING QUESTION

3–2. What is your reaction to the following statement: "If you have nothing good to say, don't say anything"?

3

Having a professional demeanor means that you are courteous, you are honest yet tactful with customers, and you put customers' interests first.

©2005 Jupiterimages Corporation

CUSTOMER SERVICE

As stated earlier, the success of any business is reflected in employee and customer satisfaction. Employee satisfaction is achieved when each employee believes that he or she is respected and appreciated by the employer. In turn, employers indicate their satisfaction with an employee's performance through formal and informal communication methods. Employers who openly communicate employees' importance to the organization discover that employees feel positively about the company and are likely to pass on those feelings to the company's customers.

"Customer service is key to any successful business that deals with the public or even in a business-to-business environment" (Stovall, 2002, p. 1). Regardless of whether the communication with the customer is by phone, in person, or in writing, good customer service skills are essential to any company's success. When customers feel respected and appreciated by a business, they are loyal to that business, which, in turn, establishes repeat business from customers. A company's value is measured both by the quality of its products and by the way it treats each customer.

A large part of demonstrating respect for customers is interacting with them in a professional manner, which is conveyed by your appearance, demeanor, and behavior. General guidelines for professional dress stipulate clean, neat clothing that follows the stipulations of your company's dress code. For example, if you work in a setting where casual dress is acceptable, your clothing can be casual, but it should be tidy and well cared for. You, like your clothing, must also be clean and well groomed.

Having a professional demeanor means that you are courteous and honest yet tactful with customers, and you put their interests first. Professional demeanor when dealing with customers is demonstrated through the behaviors noted in the following list (Loeffler, 2003):

▶ **Make a good first impression.** Whether the communication is by phone, in person, or in writing, demonstrate professionalism and courtesy through your choice of words. For example, use a formal title, such as Ms. Smith or Dr. Jones. Do not use first names unless instructed to do so by your company or the customer. Use common courtesies, such as saying "please" and "thank you." Be respectful of the caller's time by avoiding or minimizing wait times. Offer as much information as you can within appropriate guidelines and offer to research information that you do not have immediately available. Follow up with the caller.

▶ **Let customers know they are valuable during your exchanges.** Customers want to know they are more than just a number and that they are individually valued. Learn what the customer needs and wants and make every effort to provide effective information and service. Meet customers' needs creatively. Assist customers in problem solving and offer suggestions and ideas. You are the expert in your field, and customers will appreciate your efforts to apply your knowledge to their interests.

▶ **Have a professional appearance.** Customers are drawn to individuals who present themselves as a professional in both attire and in conduct. Look and act professional in all of your exchanges.

▶ **Enjoy your customers.** Smile and demonstrate a genuine interest in people. Be professional and sincere, but be friendly and have fun. Use your customers' cues and responses to help you determine an appropriate level of interaction.

▶ **Discover customers' needs by utilizing good listening skills.** Use effective listening skills, such as clarifying, asking questions, and focusing on the speaker, to understand customers' needs. Applying good listening skills is a critical component of good customer service.

▶ **Develop a trusting relationship over time.** Customers return to those with whom they have developed a rapport. Build relationships with customers by being sincere and honest (even if this means not getting the sale this time), following through on what you say you will do, and using your expertise to help customers solve problems and meet their needs.

▶ **Acknowledge a customer's presence through use of good eye contact and a smile.** If you cannot leave what you are doing when a customer arrives, let the customer know you will be with him or her as soon as possible. Never ignore a customer, regardless of how busy you are.

▶ **Treat customers with respect.** Even if you are angry or frustrated about a situation, never express those feelings to a customer.

▶ **Avoid arguing with a customer, even if the customer is wrong.** Offer reasonable options within your limitations with an explanation, as appropriate. Arguing only escalates the situation. Avoid eating, drinking, or chewing gum in front of customers: If you wish to freshen your breath, use a breath mint.

▶ **Avoid making excuses or using negative phrases when working with customers.** Comments such as "It's not my job" and "I can't help you with that" can offend customers and be detrimental to business. If you are engaged in a task that cannot be interrupted, acknowledge the customer's presence and politely let the customer know you will be with him or her as soon as possible.

▶ **Ask questions to learn customers' needs.** If you do not know the answer to a customer's question or cannot resolve a problem, say so and let the customer know that you will get back to him or her as quickly as possible. Be sure to follow through, even if that requires a phone call at a later time.

▶ **Keep personal or professional frustrations to yourself.** Address these concerns with the appropriate individuals. Customers and clients expect your focus to be on them and their needs.

▶ **Do not waste customers' time.** Avoid small talk unless the customer indicates a desire for it. Most customers would rather receive quick and efficient service than chat.

▶ **Be aware of your demeanor and unspoken messages.** Avoid arrogance, a condescending attitude, rudeness, and curtness. Be aware of how you are perceived by others and strive to improve behaviors that are interpreted as negative traits.

▶ **Use professional telephone etiquette.** When placing a call, identify yourself and explain your reason for calling. Respect the recipient's time by asking whether this or another time would be better to talk. When taking an incoming call, answer using company protocol. (Follow the same guidelines for interacting in person with customers.) If you need to put a customer on hold, ask whether doing so is acceptable or offer the customer the option to call back.

---

success steps

PRACTICING PROFESSIONAL DEMEANOR

1. Make a good first impression.
2. Treat customers with value during your exchanges.
3. Have a professional appearance.
4. Enjoy your customers.
5. Use good listening skills to discover the customer's needs.
6. Develop a trusting relationship with customers over time.
7. Acknowledge a customer's presence with good eye contact and a smile.
8. Treat customers with respect.
9. Avoid arguing with a customer, even if the customer is wrong.
10. Avoid eating, drinking, or chewing gum in front of customers.

11. Avoid making excuses or using negative phrases when working with customers.

12. Ask questions to learn the customer's needs.

13. Keep personal or professional frustrations to yourself.

14. Do not waste customers' time.

15. Be aware of your demeanor and unspoken messages.

16. Use professional telephone etiquette.

BUSINESS WRITING

Effective business communication encompasses both the spoken and the written word. Those who develop the skills required to compose high-quality written business communications are more efficient and productive. Business letters, memos, and e-mails are examples of written communication that occurs in the workplace.

BUSINESS LETTERS

Business writing is effective when individuals pay attention to and incorporate the following concepts into their writing: **C**lear, **C**oncise, **C**orrect, **C**ourteous, **C**onversational, **C**onvincing, and **C**omplete, also known as "The Seven Cs of Business Letter Writing" (*Business Letter Writing,* 2003a, p. 1). In business situations, your reader's time is precious. So your correspondence must be succinct and accurate to avoid creating confusion, wasting the reader's time, or failing to achieve its goal. To help eliminate confusion, use short sentences and simple words, and avoid using wordy phrases, jargon, technical terms and abbreviations, and abstract words and phrases (*Business Letter Writing,* 2003b). Use courteous language to convey professionalism and a caring, thoughtful attitude. Carefully select your words to effectively convey important points to the reader. The information you supply must be complete enough for the reader to draw correct conclusions from the message, but be free of unnecessary details that may cause confusion.

When writing, it is critical to consider who your reader(s) is (are). "If you keep your readers in mind when you write, it will help you use the right tone, appropriate language and include the right amount of detail. If you imagine yourself in your reader's position, you're more likely to write a good letter" (*Business Letter Writing,* 2003c, p. 1). By asking the following

3

questions based on suggestions from the book *Business Letter Writing*, you will be better equipped to meet the needs and expectations of your audience.

▶ What are the backgrounds of my readers?

▶ What is their level of expertise on this subject?

▶ What additional information do they need to know?

▶ What information might be interesting for them to know?

▶ Will I need to use technical terms? If so, which ones will I need to define?

▶ What are the readers' biases and prejudices? How should I take those into consideration?

▶ What are the audiences' concerns? How should I take these into consideration?

▶ Will I need to persuade the audience to a point of view? How can I accomplish this?

▶ What reactions can I anticipate?

Professionalism is conveyed not only through your choice of words, but also through your letter's appearance. Study the following suggestions for formatting a business letter (Colorado State University, 1997–2005):

▶ The sender's contact information should be provided on the company's letterhead. The information should include the sender's name, address, and phone number. Cell phone numbers and fax numbers may also be provided.

▶ Include the recipient's company's name, reader's name and title, and address. Courtesy titles should be used when appropriate. For example, *Dr. Russell Smith.*

▶ If the reader's name is unknown, an attention line should be used. For example, *Attention: Director of Lab Department.*

▶ A subject line that indicates the content of the letter may be used. For example, *Subject: Time Sheets.*

▶ A salutation should always be used in a business letter. The typical salutation is "Dear" followed by the reader's courtesy title and last name. For example, *Dear Dr. Smith.*

▶ Business letters are typically single spaced. A general rule for length is three paragraphs: an introductory paragraph, a paragraph that contains the main theme and points of the letter, and a concluding paragraph.

▶ *Sincerely, cordially,* and *yours truly* are appropriate closes for a business letter. The first word of the close is capitalized (others are not) and followed by a comma. For example, *Yours truly,*

3

▶ The writer of the letter should type his or her name and title four lines after the complimentary close. Above the typed name the writer should sign his or her name.

▶ End notations are needed if someone else has typed the letter. The end notation identifies this individual by his or her initials. For example, if Kathy Priest wrote the letter but Jan Jones typed it, the following end notations would be utilized: *KP/jj*. The end notation *Enclosure* indicates if the envelope contains any documents in addition to the letter. The word *enclosure* should be used, followed by a number indicating how many documents are present. Typically, the names of the enclosures are noted in the body of the letter. For example, *The agenda for Tuesday's meeting and the proposal for the new training program are enclosed for your review* would be included in the letter body. The end notation would appear as *Enclosure (2)*.

▶ If a copy of the letter is being sent to other readers, this is indicated in the copy line. For example, *cc: John Smith, Judith Tanker*.

Spacing requirements are standard and are indicated in the letter example presented in Figure 3–1.

MEMOS

Business memos can be simple or complex, depending on the information they convey. Typically, the purpose of a memo is to inform readers about new information, such as policy changes, price increases, and so on, or to request the reader to take an action, such as attending a meeting (Purdue University Online Writing Lab, 1995–2004). Memos generally are shorter in length than business letters. To facilitate ease of reading, consider using bullet lists when appropriate (Purdue University Online Writing Lab, 1995–2004).

A memo typically opens with the following information:

▶ TO: (recipients' names and job titles)
▶ FROM: (your name and job title)
▶ DATE: (current date)
▶ SUBJECT: (what the memo is about)

The body of the memo can include one paragraph or more, depending on the complexity of the information. The first section of the memo should clearly state its purpose by explaining the issue at hand and the related task or assignment. More in-depth information may be included as needed, such as a discussion segment that provides details supporting the stated ideas, or a summary that emphasizes the memo's main points. The second section of

3

Regency Center
248 Samuel Avenue
Santa Barbara, CA 92418
Telephone: 928-467-0298
Fax: 928-461-0137

May 24, 2005

Nathan Right
Right Corporation
2834 E. Smith Road
Franktown, MA 21345

Dear Mr. Right:

Thank you for your time. It was a pleasure speaking with you today. Enclosed are some promotional materials that will help further acquaint you with our facilities and services.

In regards to your upcoming company event, we are looking forward to the opportunity to provide you with the quality of service that Regency Center offers to their customers.

Once you have reviewed the enclosed information, we look forward to speaking with you further regarding how we might be of service.

Thank you for choosing the Regency Center.

Sincerely,

Sara Duncun
Promotions Manager, Regency Center
928-467-0297
sduncan@pm.regencycenter.com

Enclosure (3)

FIGURE 3–1.   A business letter requires professional wording and attention to details such as spacing and appearance. Figure 3–1 is an example of a professionally written letter that illustrates the appropriate spacing.

the memo should clearly state what steps the reader is to take. In addition, explain the benefits of the action and provide information about any support that is available to the reader to help him or her achieve the stated goals. For lengthier assignments or in situations where more extensive information is required, an attachment (similar to an attachment to a business letter) may be used. If an attachment is provided, include the following notation at the end of the memo: *Attached: [Name of the attachment]* (Purdue University Online Writing Lab, 1995–2004).

As with a business letter, make sure to adhere to the "Seven Cs." An example of a memo can be found in Figure 3-2.

MEMORANDUM

TO: Brent Lloyd

COPIES TO: Jon Dwight, Chris Marshall

FROM: Jane Lucy (her signed initials would go next to her name)

DATE: May 24, 2006

SUBJECT: New Construction

Brent, we have just been informed that your department will be under new construction starting on June 1, 2005 and will last for about 4 days.

We are sorry for the inconvenience but once the new construction is completed the new equipment for your department will be installed.

Please inform your staff and address any arrangements that must be made to accommodate your staff during this time. If any assistance is needed to make these arrangements, please let me know.

FIGURE 3–2. Although less formal than a business letter, a business memo also must meet certain criteria. Figure 3–2 illustrates the appropriate format for a business memo.

3

E-MAILS

E-mail has significantly impacted workplace communication among employees, among businesses, and between businesses and their customers. Today, fewer business letters and memos are created, while the use of e-mail continues to increase, and the appropriate use of e-mail can save time and expense. As with the traditional forms of written business communication, however, e-mail has its own set of standards. Study the following suggestions for using e-mail appropriately and effectively (Brody, 2005):

▶ **Keep e-mails brief, concise, and to the point.** Strive to keep the entire message visible in the window that appears when you click the *Compose new message* button (or whatever "new message" button your e-mail software uses). If it is necessary to provide lengthy support information, include it as an attachment. Be aware that large attachments take longer to download and take up more space on the recipient's hard drive. Faxing lengthy documents is an alternative to sending them as e-mail attachments.

▶ **Address one topic per message.** Doing so allows recipients to focus on a single issue as well as to file e-mails according to topic. Considering the amount of information received daily via e-mail, including one topic per message maximizes the effectiveness of your e-mail.

▶ **Avoid being antagonistic or critical.** Online, this behavior is known as "flaming." Constructive criticism or corrective comments are more appropriately done in person. Do not use words presented in all capital letters, as this is the e-mail equivalent of shouting.

▶ **Ensure that all e-mails you send have value for the recipient.** If messages lack value, they may be considered "spam" and deleted. When you send jokes and similar content, you stand the risk of losing credibility with professional colleagues and of violating your company's computer use policy. Use judgment regarding what you send.

▶ **Be aware that there is no such thing as a private e-mail.** Information technology (IT) staff can use software and online services to access messages even after they have been deleted.

▶ **Check spelling and punctuation for accuracy.** E-mail correspondence is sometimes considered to be less formal than hard-copy correspondence, but e-mail messages should follow the same rules

success steps

COMPOSING EFFECTIVE E-MAILS

1. Keep e-mails brief, concise, and to the point.
2. Address one topic per e-mail.
3. Avoid being antagonistic or critical.
4. Ensure that all e-mails you send have value for the recipient.
5. Be aware that there is no such as a private e-mail.
6. Check spelling and punctuation for accuracy.
7. Include a meaningful subject line.
8. Respond to e-mails within 24 hours.
9. Communicate your unavailability.

REFLECTION QUESTIONS

- What is the quality of your writing skills? What areas of writing do you find challenging?
- Do you ever find receiving e-mails annoying? If so, what about it is annoying? How can you make sure your e-mails do not irritate or annoy others?

CRITICAL THINKING QUESTION

3–3. How can miscommunications occur with e-mail and how can these miscommunications be avoided?

of clarity and correctness as other correspondence. Most e-mail software has a spelling and grammar check. Use these tools if they are available, but realize that they catch only certain errors. You should carefully proofread your message before sending it, just as you would any other letter.

▶ **Include a meaningful subject line.** A relevant subject line that conveys the main point of the e-mail allows busy professionals to organize and prioritize their messages.

▶ **Respond to e-mails within 24 hours.** Doing so is considered professional and courteous. If you need more time to compose an in-depth answer or retrieve information, make this clear in your reply.

▶ **Communicate your unavailability.** Let people know if you will not be checking e-mail for an extended period of absence, such as during a vacation. Use the automated "out of office" reply that lets senders know that you are away and when you plan to return.

CHAPTER SUMMARY

Communication is a critical factor in professional success. This chapter introduced elements of communication that contribute to effective relationships with colleagues and customers. Listening skills were emphasized as

3

a major factor in resolving conflict, hearing corrective feedback, and in other professional interactions.

POINTS TO KEEP IN MIND

In this chapter, several main points were discussed in detail:

▶ Your satisfaction at work greatly relies on your ability to use effective communication skills.

▶ Communicating effectively with others leads to increased employee satisfaction and productivity.

▶ Communication is successful only if all parties involved clearly understand the message that is being conveyed.

▶ Listening is a critical factor to effective communication.

▶ The success of any business is reflected in employee and customer satisfaction.

▶ The influence of satisfying interactions between employer and employee is reflected in communications with customers.

▶ Learning how to get along with others is important for overall career success.

▶ Employees can de-escalate conflict in a variety of ways.

▶ Regardless of whether communication with the customer is by phone, in person, or in writing, effective customer service skills must be demonstrated.

▶ The manner in which one deals with criticism makes a significant statement regarding one's desire to grow personally and professionally.

▶ Your reader's time is precious, so information must be communicated clearly, concisely, and correctly.

▶ When writing, it is critical to consider who your reader(s) is (are) and to adjust your tone, language, and amount of detail accordingly.

▶ Correct use of the various elements of a business letter, its appearance, and word choice all contribute to a professional image.

apply it

Writing a Business Letter

GOAL: To develop a better understanding of the content of a business letter.

STEP 1: Write a business letter utilizing the various elements discussed on pages 58–59.

STEP 2: Submit the first draft of the letter to the instructor to be reviewed. Have the instructor provide feedback regarding areas that can be improved and rewrite the letter for a final submission.

STEP 3: Consider placing the business letter in your Learning Portfolio.

3

apply it

Handling Criticism

GOAL: To help develop a deeper understanding of how to handle criticism effectively.

STEP 1: Divide the class into pairs. In each pair, one student should take the role of "supervisor," and the other the role of "employee."

STEP 2: Each "employee" should perform a short task that the "supervisor" will critique.

STEP 3: After the "supervisor" has critiqued the performance/task, the "employee" should respond to how he or she felt about what was said and how it was said. (The "employee" is actually critiquing the critique.) Have the "supervisor" respond to what has been shared. When the exercise is complete, the students should switch roles and repeat the exercise.

3

apply it

Web Research Report

GOAL: *To gain further understanding of topics discussed in this chapter.*

STEP 1: Conduct further research on at least one topic from this chapter.

STEP 2: Write a brief report on what Web sites you used in your research and what you learned.

STEP 3: Consider placing this report in your Learning Portfolio.

LEARNING OBJECTIVES REVISITED

Review the learning objectives for this chapter and rate your level of achievement for each objective using the rating scale provided. For each objective on which you do not rate yourself as a 3, outline a plan of action that you will take to fully achieve the objective. Include a time frame for this plan.

1 = did not successfully achieve objective

2 = understand what is needed, but need more study or practice

3 = achieved learning objective thoroughly

	1	2	3
Define *communication* and explain when communication is viewed as successful.	☐	☐	☐
Discuss what is involved in achieving effective verbal communication.	☐	☐	☐
Describe how effective listening can be achieved.	☐	☐	☐
Explain methods to increase strong internal communication between employers and employees.	☐	☐	☐
Discuss how to establish and maintain positive relationships in the workplace.	☐	☐	☐
Explain how conflict can be de-escalated.	☐	☐	☐

Discuss how employee satisfaction is reflected
in customer satisfaction. □ □ □

Describe the do's and don'ts of customer service. □ □ □

List and explain the steps involved in responding to
criticism. □ □ □

List and explain the Seven Cs of effective business writing. □ □ □

Discuss the general format of a business letter. □ □ □

Explain the basic format of a memo. □ □ □

Discuss issues to consider when using e-mail and composing
e-mail in the workplace. □ □ □

Steps to Achieve Unmet Objectives

Steps   Due Date

1. _____   _____

2. _____   _____

3. _____   _____

4. _____   _____

SUGGESTED ITEMS FOR LEARNING PORTFOLIO

Refer to the "Developing Portfolios" section at the front of this textbook for more information on learning portfolios.

- ▶ Business Letter: This activity will give you experience writing an effective business letter.

- ▶ Web Research Report: Use this activity to explore a topic discussed in this chapter that you would like to learn more about.

- ▶ Handling Criticism: Write in your journal about your responses to this activity to help you develop your skills in using feedback effectively.

REFERENCES

Accel-Team. (2004a). Business communications: Conceptual model [electronic version]. Retrieved May 5, 2005, from http://www.accel-team.com/communications/busComms_00.html

Accel-Team. (2004b). Business communications: Why all this fuss about listening [electronic version]. Retrieved May 5, 2005, from http://www.accel-team.com/communications/busComms_02.html

Anderson, K. (n.d.). Handling criticism with honesty and grace [electronic version]. *Speaker's Platform*. Retrieved May 5, 2005, from http://www.speaking.com/articles_html/KareAnderson_622.html

Anderson, K. (2004). Resolving everyday conflicts sooner [electronic version]. Retrieved May 5, 2005, from http://www.pertinent.com/articles/communication/kareCom91.asp

Brody, M. (2005). Rules for the wired: Effective customer service in an age of electronic communication [electronic version]. *4Hoteliers: Hospitality and Travel News*. Retrieved May 5, 2005, from http://www.4hoteliers.com/4hots_fshw.php?mwi=518

Business Letter Writing. (2003a). The seven Cs of business letter writing [electronic version]. Retrieved May 6, 2005 from http://www.business-letter-writing.com/writing-a-business-letter-examples/7Cs-of-business- . . .

Business Letter Writing. (2003b). Writing your business plan in plain English [electronic version]. Retrieved May 6, 2005, from http://www.business-letter-writing.com/writing-a-business-letter-examples/writing-your-bus . . .

Business Letter Writing. (2003c). Putting your reader first [electronic version]. Retrieved May 6, 2005, from http://www.business-letter-writing.com/writing-a-business-letter-examples/putting-your-rea . . .

Colorado State University. (1997–2005). Writing@CSU: Writing guides. Introduction: business letters [electronic version]. Retrieved May 6, 2005, from http://writing.colostate.edu/references/documents/bletter

Loeffler, B. (2003–2005). Good service: A matter of "do's and don'ts" [electronic version]. Retrieved May 5, 2005, from http://www.enspiron.cc/article.asp?ID=28

McNamara, C. (1999). Free basic guide to leadership and supervision: Basics of internal communications [electronic version]. Retrieved May 5, 2005, from http://www.mapnp.org/library/mgmnt/prsnlmnt.htm

Purdue University Online Writing Lab. (1995–2004). Memo writing [electronic version]. Retrieved May 6, 2005, from http://owl.english .purdue.edu/handouts/pw/p_memo.html

Stovall, J. (2002). Customer service [electronic version]. Retrieved May 5, 2005, from http://refresher.com/!jsservice.html

Waughfield, C. G. (2002). *Mental Health Concepts* (5th ed.). Clifton Park, NY: Thomson-Delmar, a division of Thomson Learning, Inc.

3

CHAPTER OUTLINE

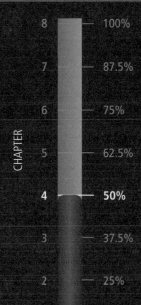

4 Information Skills

THE BIG PICTURE

CHAPTER		
8		100%
7		87.5%
6		75%
5		62.5%
4		**50%**
3		37.5%
2		25%
1		12.5%

LEARNING OBJECTIVES

By the end of this chapter, you will achieve the following objectives:

▶ Define *information literacy.*

▶ Explain the importance of information literacy in today's workplace and articulate its relationship to professional expectations.

▶ Summarize standards for information literacy competency as defined by the Association of College and Research Libraries (ACRL).

▶ Describe characteristics of individuals who are competent in informational literacy.

▶ Implement strategies for developing information-literacy competencies for the workplace.

▶ Identify sources of professional information and describe mechanisms for obtaining information from these sources.

▶ Evaluate information effectively based on specified criteria.

4

TOPIC SCENARIO

Janelle has been charged with researching inventory management software for her company. Her supervisor has provided her with the criteria for the software's functionality and cost. Janelle is not a software expert, but she has basic knowledge of what is needed.

Based on this scenario, answer the following questions:

▶ What elements should Janelle consider in beginning her research?

▶ What is important for Janelle to know about inventory management software?

▶ From what sources might she gather relevant information? (List as many as you can think of.)

▶ How will she evaluate the information to ensure its accuracy and relevance?

INFORMATION LITERACY: AN OVERVIEW

Information literacy is emphasized as a skill necessary for effective job performance, according to the United States Department of Labor Secretary's Commission on Achieving Necessary Skills (SCANS); other countries have also emphasized the importance of information literacy (Cheuk, 2002). The purpose of this chapter is to introduce the concept of information literacy, ways to develop it, and define its importance in today's workplace.

WHAT IS INFORMATION LITERACY?

Information literacy is the ability to recognize the need for information; know the type of information needed; and be able to locate, organize, and evaluate it effectively. In addition to retrieving and using information productively, information literacy includes the ability to develop and present information effectively to its intended audience (Association of College & Research Libraries [ACRL], 2000; Cheuk, 2002). In short, being information literate means being able to use information from a variety of sources to respond to situations appropriately and effectively.

THE IMPORTANCE OF INFORMATION LITERACY

Today, the speed with which we communicate and the rate at which knowledge becomes available make information literacy a critical skill for the

©BananaStock Ltd.

The ability to locate and use a variety of information is critical to your career success.

workplace. The Internet and other global communications systems have greatly increased access to information, creating a corresponding need to quickly process it, make decisions about it, and exercise flexibility when dealing with it. Technology has increased the pace of research and development, requiring a continual readiness to adapt to change. Your ability to use, process, and evaluate information has a direct bearing on your capacity to function efficiently.

In addition to the quantity of information and the rate at which it is received, the variety of media (auditory, graphical, electronic, and hard copy, to name a few) requires proficiency in using a variety of formats to obtain information (ACRL, 2000). Being able to use various media for retrieving and presenting information, as well as having a basic understanding of the technology needed for doing so, is critical.

Regardless of the rate at which or the format in which information is received, making wise choices about the information you need and use is critical to your success. Information comes from numerous sources (many of which are unfiltered), so it is essential to be able to judge its quality and legitimacy (Cheuk, 2002). You must ensure that information comes from reliable sources and be able to think critically about the information that you receive and use.

INFORMATION LITERACY AND LIFELONG LEARNING

Your college education is just the beginning of your professional learning. To remain knowledgeable and current in your field, you must stay informed of the new information and developments in your profession. Information literacy is an essential element of lifelong learning in that it provides a foundation for your professional development by decreasing your dependence on others as sources and interpreters of information. Being information literate enables you to direct your own learning and decision making (ACRL, 2000).

INFORMATION-LITERACY COMPETENCY

The Association of College and Research Libraries (ACRL) has developed a set of standards for information literacy competency, emphasizing that these standards apply across all disciplines in both academic and professional venues (ACRL, 2000). The five standards are listed here and described according to the performance indicators and outcomes defined by the ACRL.

"The information literate student determines the nature and extent of the information needed": An individual who has met this competency recognizes the need for information, is able to name sources for obtaining it, and is aware of the cost to benefit ratio of obtaining and using various forms of information. This individual evaluates the amount and type of

REFLECTION QUESTION

• How do you see information-literacy skills benefiting you in your chosen career?

4

information that is needed and selects ample and effective resources without overwhelming the audience with extraneous information.

"The information literate student assesses needed information effectively and efficiently": This competency includes being able to access information in various formats, using a variety of technologies, and selecting the most appropriate and efficient retrieval method or activity. This competency includes the ability to devise effective search and search refinement strategies (both on- and offline) and the ability to organize and manage retrieved information.

"The information literate student evaluates information and its sources critically and incorporates selected information into his or her knowledge base and value system": The individual who has achieved this competency has the ability to review and evaluate multiple sources, understand them conceptually, and synthesize the main ideas into original concepts and hypotheses. This individual presents work in his or her own words while representing facts accurately, using verbatim quotes appropriately, and citing sources according to recommended protocol. Information is interpreted according to context, value systems, and other relevant factors.

"The information literate student, individually or as a member of a group, uses information effectively to accomplish a specific purpose": Achieving this competency indicates that the individual is able to use information appropriately to achieve a specific outcome or generate a product, evaluates and modifies the process on a continual basis, and presents outcomes effectively to the intended audience.

"The information literate student understands many of the economic, legal, and social issues surrounding the use of information and accesses information ethically and legally": This individual understands the ethical and legal issues related to plagiarism, confidentiality, copyright, and similar concerns. This individual honors laws and policies related to information use and uses appropriate communication skills and etiquette in online and on ground (classroom) environments.

For more detailed information regarding specific outcomes based on these standards, you are encouraged to access the full document at ACRL's Web site at http://www.acri.org.

? CRITICAL THINKING QUESTIONS

4–1. How effective are your information-literacy skills? (Be as specific as possible in your answer.)

4–2. In what areas can you improve?

4–3. What steps can you take and what activities can you do to develop your skills?

©Digital Vision

Using information in various formats and collaboratively with colleagues makes you a more effective professional.

apply it

Assessing Your Information Literacy

GOAL: *To assess your information-literacy skills and set goals for its development.*

STEP 1: Create a three-column table in an electronic or paper document. Label the first column "Competency"; the second,

"Assessment"; and the third, "Goals and Methods." In a separate document, create a page (or pages) and label it (or them) "Tips and Ideas."

STEP 2: Using the competencies outlined by the Association of College and Research Libraries, list the competencies for information literacy in the left-hand column. Note that the competencies presented in this chapter reflect major categories. If you desire more detailed descriptions, follow the ACRL Web site's ad link to the information competencies document.

STEP 3: Make an honest assessment of your skills related to each competency and record your findings in the "Assessment" column. In the third column, write specific and measurable goals to develop your skills information-literacy skills.

STEP 4: Record ideas for streamlining your use of information on the "Tips and Ideas" sheet. Also include reflections, suggestions, and other thoughts that you have.

STEP 5: Consider placing both documents in your Learning Portfolio.

4

STRATEGIES FOR DEVELOPING INFORMATION-LITERACY COMPETENCY FOR THE WORKPLACE

There are recommended strategies for applying to professional activities information-literacy competencies for obtaining, organizing, and presenting information. Study the following strategies suggested by Bonnie Wai-Yi Cheuk (2002), information manager at Arthur Andersen:

▶ **Determine where information is lacking.** Review the information that you already have that is relevant to your task. Determine what, if any, information is missing and identify areas that need expansion. For example, if you are charged with demonstrating the cost effectiveness of a proposed program, review of your data may indicate a need for additional information that illustrates how similar projects in other companies have contributed to the bottom line.

▶ **Determine the best resources and processes for obtaining needed information.** There are numerous sources of information. Each has its own advantages and disadvantages, depending on your situation and the goals of your task. Selecting the most appropriate

4

resource for your needs can add credibility and validity to your project. To continue with the example of demonstrating cost effectiveness cited previously, an effective source of information might be interviews with directors of similar programs who can offer testimonials regarding the advantages of certain resources. In this situation, input from professional colleagues in a similar business may be more effective than a report from an unknown entity retrieved from the Internet.

▶ **Locate, retrieve, and review the information.** After you have determined the most appropriate information source for your task, the information must be retrieved, reviewed, and evaluated. Being knowledgeable of library systems, electronic search techniques, and methods for contacting human resources is critical to locating and retrieving information. To continue with the example of demonstrating cost effectiveness, you need to be able to determine which businesses and individuals to contact, be able to effectively interview or correspond with them to obtain the information, and be able to review it promptly and effectively to determine whether any follow-up or clarification is needed. At this step, your knowledge of confidentiality, copyright, and other legal and ethical considerations will allow you to treat the information within the limits of the law and ethical codes of conduct.

▶ **Evaluate the information that you find.** Analysis of the information that you obtain maximizes its credibility by ensuring that the information is relevant to your task. It is important to critically analyze information for its validity and reliability so that it effectively supports your goals. Analyze information for its relevance to your purpose; its accuracy, reliability, and validity; and its appropriateness for your intended audience.

▶ **Organize the information logically according to your purpose or task.** Organize your information so that it is presented in a manner that builds logically to support your purpose. Begin with basic information that provides a foundation for your discussion or proposal. Next, demonstrate how it applies to your task or purpose.

▶ **Make interpretations and draw conclusions.** Take your information beyond general facts. Synthesize data from a variety of sources to create solutions and present new ideas. Generate new thoughts, supporting them with these facts. Use statistics appropriately and make sure any statistics that you cite show an accurate correlation. For example, it may be possible to show a statistical correlation between drownings and eating ice cream. However, it is also possible that the correlation exists because there are more people swimming and eating ice cream in the summer, so the frequency of both events will rise. Ensure that your interpretations and conclusions are logical and reflect substantial and verifiable relationships.

▶ **Present the finished product to stakeholders.** Part of information-literacy competency is the ability to use a variety of presentation methods and select from your repertoire one that best supports the information you are presenting and meets the needs of your audience. To accomplish this effectively, it is important to consider the format (for example, textual, graphical, or aural) as well as the type of media (for example, video, recording, verbal presentation, or a combination). The selection of appropriate format and media type can greatly enhance the effectiveness of your presentation.

▶ **Evaluate the process.** Upon conclusion of these steps, it is critical to evaluate the process to determine its effectiveness and to identify any changes that can be made to improve it. If you notice a problem, identify the step (for example, determining needed information or evaluating information) where the problem originated and assess that step in greater detail to determine the precise issue. If there are no identifiable problems, assessment is still important to determine strategies for general improvement as well as to identify aspects of the process that were effective and will be useful in the future.

success steps

STRATEGIES FOR PRACTICING INFORMATION LITERACY

1. Determine where information is lacking.
2. Determine the best resources and processes for obtaining needed information.
3. Locate, retrieve, and review the information.
4. Evaluate the information that you find.
5. Organize the information logically according to your purpose or task.
6. Make interpretations and draw conclusions.
7. Present the finished product to stakeholders.
8. Evaluate the process.

apply it

Developing Presentation Skills

GOAL: To expand your ability to present information effectively.

STEP 1: Identify a format (textual, graphical, or aural) and a media (electronic, print, or presentation) with which you want to become more proficient. For example, if you want to develop your ability to use PowerPoint, it will become the focus of this activity. Another example is increasing your ability to incorporate images into written material.

STEP 2: Research ways in which to use the format and media that you select. You may refer to textbooks or seek assistance from a qualified individual.

STEP 3: Create a presentation of information using the format and media that you select. Consider incorporating this into a class assignment or create a project solely for the purpose of this activity.

STEP 4: Present your information and request feedback on the effectiveness of the presentation.

STEP 5: Consider placing your project and feedback in your learning portfolio.

Numerous information sources, including the library or learning resource center, are available on your college campus.

SOURCES OF PROFESSIONAL INFORMATION

A significant part of being information literate is the ability to locate and retrieve valid information. There are numerous sources for obtaining information, and each has its advantages and disadvantages. Consider the following sources that may be available to you. You may have additional sources, depending on your location and profession.

CAMPUS RESOURCES

Your college campus is a significant resource for information, offering a variety of print, electronic, and human resources. Some colleges make selected resources available to graduates; check to see what facilities you might be able to access as an alumnus.

College Library or Learning Resource Center

College libraries typically house a greater variety of professional journals and other publications than do public libraries. Be aware that professional journals may contain articles not available via the Internet or in other popular publications. In addition, college libraries frequently subscribe to information services such as Thomson's Infotrac, which provides access to thousands of professional articles.

Faculty and Staff

College faculty and staff can often provide expertise on various topics within their field. For example, an instructor in a computer science program may have in-depth knowledge of a certain software program, as well as have ideas for obtaining additional resources on it. Human resources such as faculty members and other subject experts may be interviewed for firsthand information.

apply it

Information Tour

GOAL: To become familiar with information sources and their purposes.

STEP 1: Contact your school librarian or the director of your learning resource center. Request an orientation to the information resources available on the Internet, in professional journals, and from other sources.

STEP 2: Assemble a group of students who also are invested in developing their information literacy skills.

STEP 3: Consider repeating this activity in your public library.

STEP 4: Consider placing information and guidelines that you receive in your Learning Portfolio.

THE INTERNET

The Internet provides a wealth of information from a variety of sources. Consider the following online sources.

▶ **Using Search Engines**
Search engines are the mechanisms that find Web sites relevant to the search term you use. Organizations, individuals, and businesses register their sites with search engines and often pay a fee to have their sites accessible through a particular search engine. A metacrawler, or metasearch, engine relays your search term to several search engines and compiles the results from each to give

4

you a comprehensive list of resources. To make searches more specific, follow the instructions for advanced searching on the search engine you use.

▌ **Using Directories**
Directories are listings of resources specific to a field or area of interest. Consider print directories, such as a telephone directory or neighborhood business directory, as examples. There are numerous online directories for a variety of resources in different areas, including those of professionals and organizations in a specific field, article listings, and other information focused in a specific area. To find a directory of resources for your task or area of interest, conduct an Internet search using your discipline plus the word "directory." For example, if you are seeking ballet company directories, enter "ballet company directories" as your search term.

▌ **Accessing the Deep Web**
The deep Web contains links to sites and information that is typically not found with common search engines. This information is generally found in some type of database, as an image or media file, or as a .pdf (portable document format), Word, or other software application file. Some of the resources are free, while you may be charged for using others. To find specific tools to access information from the deep Web, enter "the deep Web" as your search term in your usual search engine. Explore the tools that are accessed as a result of your search.

▌ **Searching for Images**
Most commonly used search engines have image banks that contain images from numerous areas and disciplines. To access these resources, click on "Images" from your search engine's home page. From the Images page, enter your search term as you would for a general Web search. You may also elect the Advanced Search option, which allows you to narrow your search by using the same symbols and terms as you would to conduct a more specific general search.

▌ **Accessing Virtual Museums and Exhibits**
Virtual museums are online versions of exhibits and displays found in traditional, "bricks-and-mortar" museums. Online museums provide an opportunity to view exhibits that are not located near you. Some of these online programs offer tours of well-known museums, such as the Louvre Museum in Paris, as well as of exhibits from smaller museums. The latter can focus on various topics, some of which may be obscure. Find a variety of virtual museums by conducting a search using the phrase "virtual museums _____" (fill in your area of interest).

Information from the Internet must be evaluated for its source, its accuracy, and its reliability.

▶ Using Simulations

Simulations are virtual situations that allow the user to experience a situation similar to authentic circumstances. For example, astronauts in training use simulations to replicate the conditions of shuttle flights, which allows the astronauts to practice their skills in a safe environment before their actual flight. Technology has made it possible for the general public to experience simulations via the Web, and you may be able to find simulations relevant to your field. If your information is best conveyed by demonstration, simulations provide an excellent resource for practice. To find simulations in your field, conduct a search by using the search term "simulations" or "simulations in _____" (fill in your field of interest).

Evaluating Internet Information

Although the Internet is a convenient and ever-expanding source of information, it is also unregulated. It is critical that you analyze information found on the Internet and assess it by evaluating its source and that source's credibility, determining whether the information is fact or opinion, and considering whether the information represents special interests. Study the following recommendations for evaluating information found on the Internet (Kirk, 1996):

▶ **Authorship.** The author of the material should be a recognized expert in his or her field. You can determine an author's background

4

by reading available biographical information, being familiar with his or her previous works, or by knowing the author's general reputation. If you have no information about the author, contact the publisher or author for additional information. You may also assess an author's credibility based on whether he or she was recommended to you by a source known to be reliable or if you found the author's work by linking from another credible site.

▶ **The publisher.** Organizations that publish information typically employ a process of review that ensures the accuracy and relevancy of material that they publish. When assessing information, consider the publishing organization to determine whether it is recognized as well as qualified to publish within your field. Verify that the document is obtained from an identifiable server versus a personal Web site and that the author has a clear relationship with the publishing organization.

▶ **Special interests and biases.** Assess information for political, commercial, philosophical, or other special interests. Remember that information is rarely without bias. While it is not always possible to eliminate bias, it is critical to understand the impact of bias on information and, subsequently, your task. Consider the affiliations and focus of the organizations from which you retrieve your information. Typically, corporate organizations have commercial interests, and special-interest organizations have information that directly or subtly supports their cause. Scholarly publications typically are less biased, but should be supported by a credible organization or learning institution and founded in valid and reliable research.

▶ **References and timeliness.** Review the references and sources for any information that you use. References should reflect current and qualified sources for information in your field. Look for a copyright date or notation of the most recent update. Judge how current the information needs to be in order to be credible. For example, if you are discussing technology, it is important to have the most current information because technology is continually and rapidly changing.

PROFESSIONAL ORGANIZATIONS

Professional organizations are usually excellent resources for obtaining current information regarding various aspects of your field. Because a professional organization's sole focus is the field the organization represents, information from such organizations is typically current and accurate. Professional organizations have various mechanisms for disseminating information, including publications, special-interest sections and focus groups, seminars and conferences, contact people, and other resources. Research your field's professional organization to determine what information resources are available to you.

COMMUNITY RESOURCES

Become familiar with the information resources that your community offers. Resources such as libraries and nonprofit organizations are common in most areas, and you may find others specific to your locale.

Explore information resources in your community.

Public Libraries

Although public libraries tend to focus on popular publications and material geared to the general public, many offer access to the Internet and to specialty information systems such as databases. In addition, public libraries participate in interlibrary loan programs and can usually get specialty information from various sources. When using interlibrary loan, be aware that obtaining material through it can take several weeks and that the resource may need to be returned relatively quickly. Reference librarians are, themselves, a wonderful resource. They can provide you with information about interlibrary loan, assist you in using other methods to access information, and recommend additional sources.

Specialty Libraries

Specialty libraries include those housed in facilities such as hospitals and other institutions. Specialized schools, such as colleges of law or medicine, often have libraries containing materials specific to their disciplines. Some of these libraries are not open to the public, but may make special considerations for individuals in the field or be able to work with your public library to get the information to you. If you choose to use a specialty library, contact its staff to learn what options are available to you.

Professional Contacts

Professionals in your field can be excellent sources of information. Professional organizations can often put you in contact with individuals who are knowledgeable in a particular area. Or, you may already be in contact with professionals who can be information sources. Obtain information from human resources through interviews and correspondence. The individual being interviewed should be made aware of the purpose of the interview and how the information will be used. The individual's confidentiality must be honored and his or her time must be considered—as with other types of information interviews, 20 to 30 minutes is an appropriate interview length.

Nonprofit Organizations

Nonprofit organizations, such as medical societies and service organizations (for example, the American Heart Association or Rotary Clubs), can also be sources of information. Medical societies frequently have access to current research and related activities, and service organizations are typically informed about current community events. Be aware, however, that these organizations frequently are invested in various causes and may have specific agendas.

apply it

Information Resources File

GOAL: To compile a foundation of information sources.

STEP 1: Coordinate with other students to develop a list of professional resources. Examples include Web sites, publications, individuals, and professional organizations.

STEP 2: Ask the students to record relevant information about the resources they find. Include contact or publication information, URLs, a brief description of the information that is available, and other information that you believe would be helpful.

STEP 3: Compile the information physically, in a file or notebook, or electronically, so that group members can share and copy it as needed.

STEP 4: Consider placing these information sources in your Learning Portfolio.

Note: This activity can also be done individually.

4

REFLECTION QUESTION

- What other viable information sources in your field can you identify?

CRITICAL THINKING QUESTION

4–4. What are some criteria in your field that are important to consider when evaluating information that you find?

success steps

EVALUATING INFORMATION

1. Consider the expertise of the author.
2. Consider the reliability of the publishing organization.
3. Be aware of the influence of special interests and biases.
4. Make sure that references cited in resources are reputable.
5. Ensure that resources are current.

apply it

Developing Evaluation Skills

GOAL: To expand your ability to evaluate information effectively.

STEP 1: Select a topic to research and conduct an Internet search to locate information on that topic. Ideally, the topic you select will be related to an assignment or project on which you are working. Bookmark sites of interest or print a hard copy of the information.

STEP 2: Evaluate several sites based on the criteria presented in this chapter. Consider creating a checklist with places for comments to complete this task.

STEP 3: Write a brief analysis of the resource. Explain why it is or is not an effective source, or discuss your considerations for using it.

STEP 4: Ask a qualified person (perhaps an instructor or other knowledgeable individual) to review your assessment and provide you with feedback.

STEP 5: Consider placing your analysis and feedback that you receive in your Learning Portfolio.

4

CHAPTER SUMMARY

This chapter introduced you to the concept of information literacy, which is the ability to identify the need for specific types of information, locate the information, evaluate it, and use it to effectively support a thesis or contribute to the completion of a project. Information literacy includes the ability to select the most appropriate media and format for presenting information effectively. In addition to examining methods of developing competency in information literacy, the chapter text focused on methods for evaluating information based on specific criteria, such as authorship, publisher, the influence of bias and special interests, and the reliability of the author's information sources. In addition, you were introduced to sources of professional information such as professional and

4

nonprofit organizations, specialty and public libraries, and professionals in your field.

POINTS TO KEEP IN MIND

Several main points were discussed in detail in this chapter:

▶ Information literacy is a skill necessary for effective job performance, according to the United States Department of Labor Secretary's Commission on Achieving Necessary Skills.

▶ Information literacy is the ability to recognize the need for information; know the type of information needed; and be able to locate, organize, and evaluate it effectively. In addition to retrieving and using information productively, information literacy includes the ability to develop and present information effectively to its intended audience.

▶ The speed with which we communicate and the rate at which knowledge becomes available makes information literacy a critical skill for the workplace.

▶ It is critical to be able to use various media for retrieving and presenting information, as well as having a basic understanding of the technology needed for doing so.

▶ Your ability to use, process, and evaluate information has a direct bearing on your capacity to function efficiently and effectively.

▶ To remain knowledgeable and current in your field, you must stay informed of new knowledge and developments that come to the forefront of your profession.

▶ Being information literate enables you to direct your own learning and decision making.

▶ Making good choices about the information you need and use is critical to your success.

▶ It is important to organize information logically according to your purpose or task. Steps for organizing include the following:

　▶ determining the best resources and processes for obtaining needed information

　▶ locating, retrieving, and reviewing the information

　▶ evaluating the information that you find

　▶ determining where information is lacking

> ◗ making interpretations and drawing conclusions
> ◗ presenting the finished product to stakeholders
> ◗ evaluating the process

◗ The Association of College and Research Libraries has developed a set of standards for information-literacy competency and emphasizes that these standards apply across all disciplines in academic and professional venues.

◗ There are numerous sources for obtaining information, and each has advantages and disadvantages.

◗ It is critical that you analyze information found on the Internet by evaluating its source and credibility, determining whether it is fact or opinion, and considering whether it represents special interests.

LEARNING OBJECTIVES REVISITED

Review the learning objectives for this chapter and rate your level of achievement for each objective using the rating scale provided. For each objective on which you do not rate yourself as a 3, outline a plan of action that you will take to fully achieve the objective. Include a time frame for this plan.

1 = did not successfully achieve objective

2 = understand what is needed, but need more study or practice

3 = achieved learning objective thoroughly

	1	2	3
Define *information literacy*.	☐	☐	☐
Explain the importance of information literacy in today's workplace and articulate its relationship to professional expectations.	☐	☐	☐
Summarize standards for information literacy competency as defined by the Association of College and Research Libraries (ACRL).	☐	☐	☐
Describe characteristics of individuals who are competent in informational literacy.	☐	☐	☐
Implement strategies for developing information-literacy competencies for the workplace.	☐	☐	☐

Identify sources of professional information and describe mechanisms for obtaining information from these sources.   ☐ ☐ ☐

Evaluate information effectively based on specified criteria.   ☐ ☐ ☐

Steps to Achieve Unmet Objectives

Steps	Due Date
1. _____	_____
2. _____	_____
3. _____	_____
4. _____	_____

SUGGESTED ITEMS FOR LEARNING PORTFOLIO

Refer to the "Developing Portfolios" section at the front of this textbook for more information on learning portfolios.

- Assessing Your Information Literacy: This activity will help you assess your information-literacy skills and set goals for their development.

- Information Tour: This activity is intended to develop your awareness of information sources.

- Information Resources File: In this activity, you will compile a foundation of information resources.

- Developing Presentation Skills: The goal of this activity is to help you develop your presentation skills.

- Developing Evaluation Skills: This activity will help you develop effective skills for evaluating information.

REFERENCES

Association of College & Research Libraries. (2000). Information literacy competency standards for higher education [electronic version]. American Library Association, Chicago. Retrieved May 6, 2005, from http://www.ala.org/ala/acrlstandards/standards.pdf

Cheuk, B. (2002). Information literacy in the workplace context: Issues, best practices, and challenges [electronic version]. July 2002, White

Paper prepared for UNESCO, the U.S. National Commission on Libraries and Information Science, and the National Forum on Information Literacy Meeting of Experts, Prague, The Czech Republic. Retrieved May 6, 2005, from http://www.nclis.gov/libinter/infolitconf&meet/papers/cheuk-fullpaper.pdf

Kirk, E. E. (1996). Evaluating information found on the Internet [electronic version]. *John Hopkins University, The Sheridan Libraries,* 2004. Retrieved May 16, 2005, from http://www.library.jhu.edu/researchhelp/general/evaluating/

4

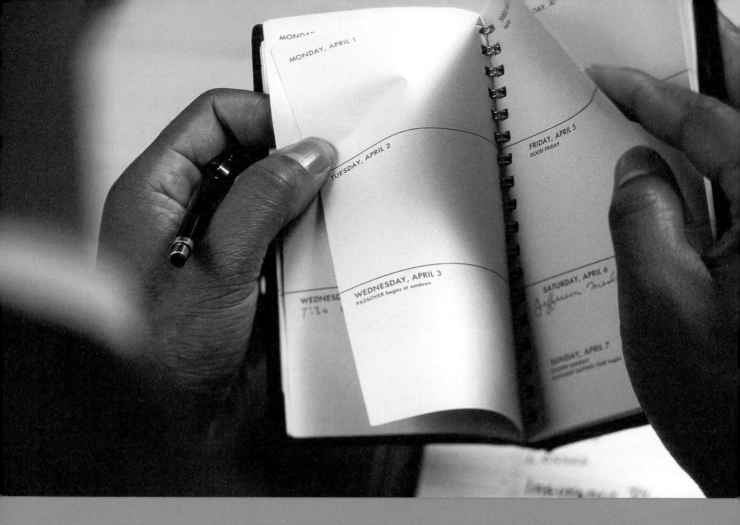

CHAPTER OUTLINE

5 Time Management

THE BIG PICTURE

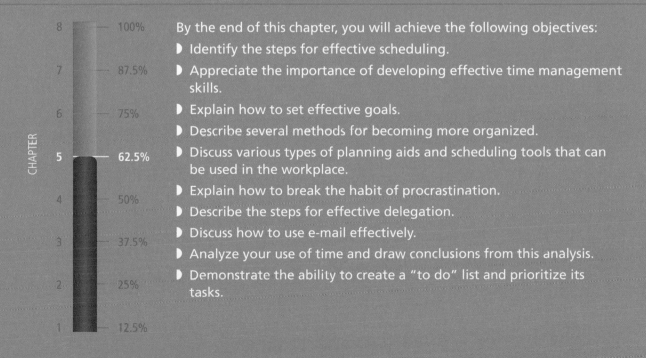

LEARNING OBJECTIVES

By the end of this chapter, you will achieve the following objectives:

▶ Identify the steps for effective scheduling.

▶ Appreciate the importance of developing effective time management skills.

▶ Explain how to set effective goals.

▶ Describe several methods for becoming more organized.

▶ Discuss various types of planning aids and scheduling tools that can be used in the workplace.

▶ Explain how to break the habit of procrastination.

▶ Describe the steps for effective delegation.

▶ Discuss how to use e-mail effectively.

▶ Analyze your use of time and draw conclusions from this analysis.

▶ Demonstrate the ability to create a "to do" list and prioritize its tasks.

Success at school and in the workplace is dependent upon effective time management skills.

5

TOPIC SCENARIO

As a recent college graduate, Jane has just started her first job in her new profession, and today is her first day. Jane just left her boss's office after having met with her to discuss Jane's work. In this meeting, Jane was informed that she will be in charge of four projects, three of which need to be completed in the next two months. Jane is already worrying about meeting the deadlines and requirements of these assignments.

Based on this short description of Jane's situation, answer the following questions:

▶ What can Jane do to alleviate some of her concerns?

▶ What should Jane, as a new employee, learn about her working environment?

▶ Should Jane voice her concerns to her boss? If so, should she wait to do this or do it now? Explain your answer.

▶ What time management tools might be important for Jane to implement?

ELEMENTS OF TIME MANAGEMENT

As students, you know that academic success is dependent on applying effective time management strategies, because balancing the demands of school, home, and work is challenging. The skills you use to manage your time in school can help you succeed in your professional life. This chapter focuses on how to effectively manage time at work by further adapting to the workplace skills you probably already use, such as organizing, planning, prioritizing, scheduling, and delegating.

The concept of time management is really that of life management (Janssen, n.d.). If you learn and practice strong time management skills, the benefits can carry over into all aspects of life by generally increasing your level of organization and productivity. Author and business consultant Daniel Janssen tells us, "The most valuable things human beings have is time. You can always get more money, but once you spend time it's gone forever." Appreciating this fact can help you to see the value of time and the importance of developing effective time management skills.

Being proactive about time management and planning ahead requires making conscious decisions regarding how your time is spent. This, in turn, requires the ability to prioritize, set goals, and select activities that achieve both goals. Conscious planning allows you to be in control of your time rather than feeling overwhelmed by having too much to do in too little time (Tufts College, 2002).

▶ REFLECTION QUESTIONS

• How effective are you at managing your time?
• In what areas can you improve?

? CRITICAL THINKING QUESTION

5–1. Because many things in life are beyond your control, does learning time management really make that much difference in your overall use of time? Explain your answer.

PRIORITIZING

The first step in managing time is knowing what merits a time commitment. For example, professional, family, and personal activities are common priorities for many people. Knowing which of these areas (or others) are most important to you allows you to set goals that support these priorities. Be aware that priorities can change and that your goals will change accordingly.

GOAL SETTING

Establishing goals guides you toward success in all areas of your life, including your career. Without having goals to direct you, you may randomly choose activities that take up your time without producing clear or desired results—goal setting provides a foundation for selecting relevant activities. On a day-to-day basis, goals contribute to successful time management by defining tasks that need to be accomplished. Tasks that are clearly defined and that have a deadline for completion allow you to map out each task on the calendar. Following your plan contributes to effective time management, which, in turn, diminishes stress, because directing and organizing your tasks can help to alleviate the feeling of being overwhelmed and disorganized.

The following are suggestions on how to set effective goals (Mind Tools, 1995–2006):

- **State your goals positively.** State goals in terms of what you will do versus what you will not do. For example, "I will eat fruit for my daily afternoon snack" is a positively stated goal, while "I will not eat candy for my daily afternoon snack" is a negatively stated goal. Goals that are stated positively provide a clearer definition of what you need to accomplish.

- **Define an observable behavior.** Clearly define the action you will take to achieve your goal. Observable action is something that can be seen by you and those around you. Using the above example, stating that you will eat fruit is observable. (Eating is observable and most people agree on what fruit is.) An example of a goal that is not observable is, "I will engage in healthy habits." The difference is that the latter goal is not concrete and is open to numerous definitions.

- **Put a time limit on your goal.** Having a time limit for goal completion serves two purposes: A time limit holds you accountable, and it allows you to break goal-related tasks into manageable chunks. For example, if you have a goal to write a proposal for your business and you set a deadline two weeks in the future, you can break the proposal-writing task into daily segments over the two-week period. This makes the task manageable and is also one of the more critical components of time management. Your time limit lets

5

you know how much time you will commit to the task and how much time you will have for other activities.

▶ **Make goals measurable.** A goal that is measurable lets you know when it is completed. For example, if you have to write a 10-page term paper, you know that when 10 pages have been completed, your goal is achieved. Having a measurable goal, like setting a time limit, also lets you know how much you need to complete each day to stay within your time budget.

▶ **Make your goals challenging, yet realistic.** Strive for the "just-right challenge." Goals should hold your interest and require you to try new things and learn new material, but they should also be within your abilities and resources. Goals that do not meet these criteria are less likely to be pursued and more likely to result in an unproductive use of time, thus affecting time management.

---

success steps

SETTING GOALS FOR EFFECTIVE TIME MANAGEMENT

1. State your goals positively.

2. Define an observable behavior.

3. Put a time limit on your goal.

4. Make goals measurable.

5. Make your goals challenging, yet realistic.

PLANNING

Once your goals have been defined, you must create and implement a plan for carrying them out. A "to do" list states the general tasks that you need to accomplish. An action plan focuses on a single task or objective and includes the specific actions you will take, the resources you will use, and how each step will be carried out (Mind Tools, 1995–2005b). An action plan may be written for a single task or for parts of a task. Action plans can be on a daily, weekly, or monthly basis, depending on the goal.

After you have created an action plan, a variety of planning aids are available to help you implement it. These include pocket-size planning books, electronic planners, computer programs, simple to do lists, and wall charts. It is important to select an aid that is suitable to you and that you will use. For example, if you have difficulty maintaining paper systems in an organized fashion, an electronic organizer might be your best choice. Figure 5–1 is an example of a to do list, while Figure 5–2 shows an example of an action plan, which is more detailed.

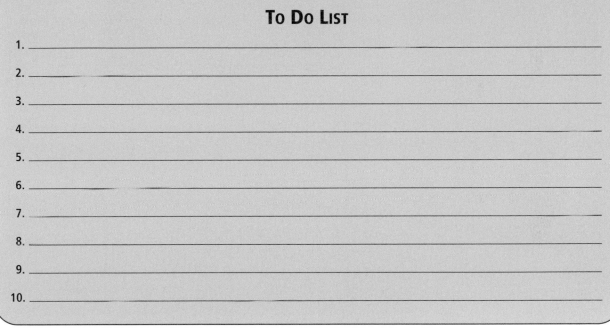

Use the following space to create a to do list of all the tasks you want to accomplish tomorrow. After you've listed them, assign each task a priority number from 1 to 4. Remember that #1 represents tasks that must be done without delay (highest priority); #2 represents tasks that should be done soon (important); #3 represents tasks that can be done next week (less important); #4 represents tasks that can be delayed for more than a week (least important). As you complete your tasks, cross them off your to do list.

TO DO LIST

1. _____
2. _____
3. _____
4. _____
5. _____
6. _____
7. _____
8. _____
9. _____
10. _____

FIGURE 5–1. A to do list allows you to prioritize tasks and organize your time based on that prioritization.

apply it

Create a To Do List and Action Plan

GOAL: To develop a to do list and prioritize each task.

STEP 1: Utilize the example of the list in Figure 5–1 to create your own to do list.

STEP 2: Divide the class into groups and have each group member share his or her list with classmates. Then, work in teams to help each other prioritize each task. Figure 5–1 can be a guide for this step.

STEP 3: Select a task from the to do list and create an action plan for it using Figure 5–2. Work in pairs to help each other develop an efficient plan.

STEP 4: Consider placing your to do list, action plan, and prioritized task list, as well as a report on creating a to do list and prioritizing tasks, in your Learning Portfolio.

REFLECTION QUESTIONS

- Does creating a to do list help you? If so, how? If not, why?
- Does creating an action plan help you? If so, how? If not, why?

The purpose of the action plan is to identify the steps and resources needed to complete a specific objective related to a goal. Use this form to identify your objective (what is to be accomplished) and complete the table to define key steps in reaching your objective.

Task Component (What needs to be done?)	Person Responsible (Who will do it?)	Resources (What is needed and where can I get it?)	Due Date	Progress Indicators (How will I know I am making progress?)	Completion Indicators (How will I know I have completed the step?)

FIGURE 5–2. An a tion plan helps you determine whi h a ti ities will a omplish a task e e ti ely and e i iently.

An efficient way to prioritize tasks is to plan to complete the most important ones first according to the goals you have set. Using a form, such as the sample one presented in Figure 5–3, may help you prioritize tasks.

ANALYZING HOW YOUR TIME IS SPENT

Regardless of how much goal setting and planning you have done, if you do not use your time wisely, you will not meet deadlines and you will fall behind in completing tasks. As a result, you run the risk of being seen as nonproductive, which creates anxiety and frustration for both you and your employer.

Analyzing how you spend your time on the job can be very enlightening. An activity log is a useful tool for enabling you to discover how you are really spending time on the job. Create an activity log by documenting every activity as each is performed, and the time spent on it. Record all work-related activities in the log, including work on specific projects, reading and writing

LIST OF TASKS FOR THE WEEK

Week of: _____

1. The tasks that must be done immediately are:

_____

_____

_____

_____

2. The tasks that are important to do soon are:

_____

_____

_____

_____

3. The tasks that can be delayed for a few days are:

_____

_____

_____

_____

4. The tasks that can be delayed for a week, a month, or longer are:

_____

_____

_____

_____

FIGURE 5–3.   se a sorting tool su h as that pi tured here to prioritize your tasks.

e-mail, and time spent socializing with coworkers. It is also helpful to note times when you feel peak energy versus times when you feel less energetic (Mind Tools, 1995–2005d). By keeping an activity log for a week or so, you can more clearly analyze where time is wisely used, where time is wasted, and the time of day when you are at your peak performance. An example of an activity log is found in Figure 5–4. Using the information documented in your activity log, use Figure 5–5 to assist you in analyzing your use of time.

Time Log

Time	Monday	Tuesday	Wednesday
7:00 a.m.			
8:00 a.m.			
9:00 a.m.			
10:00 a.m.			
11:00 a.m.			
12:00 noon			
1:00 p.m.			
2:00 p.m.			
3:00 p.m.			
4:00 p.m.			
5:00 p.m.			
6:00 p.m.			
7:00 p.m.			
8:00 p.m.			
9:00 p.m.			
10:00 p.m.			
11:00 p.m.			
12:00 midnight			
1:00 a.m.			
2:00 a.m.			
3:00 a.m.			
4:00 a.m.			
5:00 a.m.			
6:00 a.m.			

FIGURE 5–4.   Use a document such as a time log to track your activities and develop a better understanding of how your time is spent. Note time that could be used more constructively, as well as the times of day when you are most productive.

Week of _____

Thursday	Friday	Saturday	Sunday

5

5

HOW WELL I USE MY TIME

Purpose: To identify how well you use your time.

Review the time log you kept for one week and then complete the following:

1. The total number of hours I spent on these activities:

    Sleeping: _____

    Eating: _____

    Working: _____

    Attending Classes: _____

    Commuting: _____

    Studying: _____

    Chores: _____

    Exercising/Recreation: _____

    Socializing: _____

    Watching TV: _____

    Goofing Off: _____

    Other: _____

    Total should be 168 hours.

2. The total number of hours I spent on worthwhile activities:

    _____

3. The total number of hours I spent on meaningless or trivial activities:

    _____

4. The activities I wish I had spent more time on are:

    _____

    _____

    _____

    _____

    _____

    _____

5. The activities I wish I had spent less time on are:

_____

_____

_____

_____

_____

_____

6. The activities that I wanted to do but didn't get around to doing during the week are:

_____

_____

_____

_____

_____

_____

5

FIGURE 5–5.   Illustration of a method for determining where you spend your time and how you might allocate your time more effectively.

apply it

Analyzing Time

GOAL: *To increase your understanding of how you utilize time.*

STEP 1: Using the form provided in Figure 5–4, document for a week how you spend your time.

STEP 2: At the end of the week, conduct an analysis of how your time was spent, using the form provided in Figure 5–5. Write a brief report regarding what you discovered and how changes may be implemented to utilize your time more wisely.

STEP 3: Consider placing the forms and your report on analyzing time in your Learning Portfolio.

BECOMING ORGANIZED

5

The people who manage time most successfully are those who have learned how to be organized. For some individuals, organization is a skill that comes naturally due to their upbringing and their innate tendencies. For others, this skill can be quite challenging. For those of you who struggle with organizational skills, it is important to realize that the more organized you become, the more effective you will be at using time (Idaho State University, n.d.). Being disorganized in your personal life can greatly impact your professional success. For instance, both at home and at work, you can waste a significant amount of time trying to locate items amid clutter. Likewise, continually having to "reinvent the wheel" by re-creating files that you have already made but cannot find wastes valuable time. Becoming organized includes reducing clutter at home and work and putting systems and routines in place.

Becoming organized begins with developing skills at setting goals, planning, and analyzing your use of time. If you are disorganized, then establish a goal to address the disorganization and write a plan to improve your organizational skills. Consider the following suggestions for getting organized.

▶ **Break down getting organized into manageable sections.** Set a goal to complete one aspect of organization per day, such as organizing one drawer or shelf. If you are consistent with this process, your area will become organized.

▶ **Decide what you can throw or give away.** A common guideline to use when reducing clutter is that if you have not used something in a year, discard it. If items are unusable or worn, throw them away. If they are in good condition, donate them to a charitable organization. Sort the items into labeled boxes according to what is to be kept, thrown away, and donated to charity.

▶ **Identify which areas need organization.** What areas need attention? For example, if you are continually looking for pieces of clothing, then you should devise a closet organization system. If you spend too much time looking through piles of papers on your desk, then you need a filing system.

▶ **Select an organizational system.** Once you have identified the areas that need organization, devise a system. For example, if disorganized desk drawers are an issue, get a compartmentalized drawer tray. If piles of paper are your main source of clutter, sort them by project or topic into a filing system or binders. If you need suggestions for organization systems, consider one of the many books written on the subject or conduct an Internet search using "organizational skills" or "organizational systems" as your search term.

▶ **Stay organized.** Staying organized takes less time than getting organized. Once you have a system in place, get in the habit of using it consistently. For example, when you are finished with a document, return it to its file or binder. A popular guideline to help you stay organized is to touch a piece of paper one time: Look at it, determine its value, and either recycle it or file it in its proper place. The goal is to not let paper accumulate in a pile that you plan to "look at later." Return desk items to their proper places. Discipline yourself to discard items you are not using.

success steps

GETTING ORGANIZED

1. Break down getting organized into manageable sections.
2. Decide what you can throw or give away.
3. Identify the areas needing organization.
4. Select an organizational system.
5. Stay organized.

REFLECTION QUESTION

• What areas in your life do you find the most difficult to organize? How might you become more proficient at organizing this area in your life?

5

EFFECTIVE SCHEDULING

There are many elements in the work place to be scheduled, such as tasks, meetings, and staff assignments. Learning how to schedule effectively directly impacts your time management. "Scheduling is the process by which you look at the time available to you, and plan how you will use it to achieve the goals you have identified" (Mind Tools, 1995–2005d, p. 1). Those who schedule their time wisely accomplish their tasks in a timely manner with less stress. Study the following steps for effective scheduling (Mind Tools, 1995–2005d):

▶ **Identify your available time.** Block off the time you devote to professional tasks. For example, in your dayplanner or on your calendar, color code the specific times dedicated to work-related activities.

▶ **Block in essential tasks.** Identify and note tasks that are an integral part of your job and that must be completed. For example, teachers must be in class to teach at designated times. Nurses must be available to patients during specific clinic hours. These nonnegotiable commitments must be prioritized on your schedule.

Select scheduling tools suited to your needs.

▶ **Categorize other tasks.** After you have scheduled nonnegotiable commitments, sort other tasks into high, medium, and low priority. For example, tasks related to upcoming deadlines will be high priority, while research for a project coming up in the next few months will be low priority. Required "housekeeping" tasks, such as reports and correspondence, must also be categorized according to priority. For example, weekly reports and recurring tasks, such as payroll activities, must be scheduled to be completed in a timely manner.

▶ **Schedule tasks according to priority.** Schedule high-priority tasks first, medium-priority tasks second, and low-priority tasks last. You may find that low-priority tasks can be postponed and may become a higher priority later. For example, the research for the upcoming project mentioned previously will become a higher-priority task as the project deadline draws near. Incorporate the concepts of the to do list discussed earlier in this chapter to track upcoming projects.

▶ **Leave room for the unexpected.** Factor in contingency time to handle unpredictable interruptions and emergencies. If you find that this time becomes "extra" time, use it to get ahead on other tasks.

success steps

SCHEDULING EFFECTIVELY

1. Identify your available time.
2. Block in essential tasks.
3. Categorize other tasks according to their priority.
4. Schedule tasks according to their priority.
5. Leave room for the unexpected.

Many electronic and paper-based scheduling tools are available to help you plan your activities. These tools include traditional calendars, paper-based organizers in loose-leaf and bound styles, electronic personal data assistants (PDAs), and software applications such as Microsoft Outlook™. Select the format that is best suited to your needs and that you will use. For example, if you find paper systems cumbersome and inefficient, consider a PDA. A key factor in effective time management is *using* your scheduling tool. If you select a tool that is incompatible with your preferences and style, you are less likely to use it and will have greater difficulty managing your schedule. An example of a simple weekly planner is provided in Figure 5–6.

Personnel scheduling is another task performed by some employees. A variety of personnel scheduling software is available, each with various features to meet specific scheduling needs. If personnel scheduling is one of your job requirements, you will be trained in the specific scheduling process used by your organization.

apply it

Research and Presentation

GOAL: *To increase your understanding of the various types of planning or scheduling tools available.*

STEP 1: Research planning or scheduling tools.

STEP 2: Research these tools using the articles presented in this chapter (see the References section at the end of the chapter) and other resources available on the Internet and/or at the library.

STEP 3: Write a brief report on what you learned from this activity. Be prepared to make a presentation to the class.

STEP 4: Consider placing this report in your Learning Portfolio.

OVERCOMING PROCRASTINATION

Goal setting, planning, and scheduling are virtually useless if you procrastinate. Procrastination over the long term usually results in failure. People procrastinate for many reasons, including fear of failure, uncertainty about task requirements, and lack of interest. The first step to overcoming procrastination is understanding its cause; the second step is breaking the habitual cycle.

Study the following suggestions for breaking the habit of procrastination, which are based on the work of Duncan (2005a), Pavlina (2001), and Quek (2002):

▶ **Understand why you procrastinate.** Determining the reasons for your procrastination allows you to seek an effective solution. Establish why you procrastinate and address the causes accordingly. Common reasons for procrastination are listed above; you may identify additional reasons.

▶ **Seek the skills you need.** If you are faced with a task for which you may lack the skills, communicate this concern to your supervisor

Weekly Planner

Time	Monday	Tuesday	Wednesday
7:00 a.m.			
8:00 a.m.			
9:00 a.m.			
10:00 a.m.			
11:00 a.m.			
12:00 noon			
1:00 p.m.			
2:00 p.m.			
3:00 p.m.			
4:00 p.m.			
5:00 p.m.			
6:00 p.m.			
7:00 p.m.			
8:00 p.m.			
9:00 p.m.			
10:00 p.m.			
11:00 p.m.			
12:00 midnight			
1:00 a.m.			
2:00 a.m.			
3:00 a.m.			
4:00 a.m.			
5:00 a.m.			
6:00 a.m.			

FIGURE 5–6.   Use a planner such as that pictured here to map out your schedule. Many versions of planners are available in print and electronic formats.

Week of _____

Thursday	Friday	Saturday	Sunday

5

5

and find out whether delegating the work to a more qualified employee is an option. If it is not, then work closely with someone, such as your supervisor or a colleague, who can encourage you and offer helpful suggestions for completing the task.

▶ **Break down large tasks.** If the task's size is overwhelming, break it down into smaller projects. Then, write down how each smaller task will be completed and note a deadline for each task. Use the to do list and action plan concepts and your scheduling tools to accomplish this.

▶ **Prioritize deadlines.** Make meeting deadlines a priority by planning how tasks will get done. Write down the goals of the project and create a well-thought-out schedule that you can meet. Discipline yourself to complete each task in the time you have allotted for it. Meeting deadlines will make you a highly valued employee with advancement potential.

▶ **Stay focused.** Avoid anything that distracts you from the task that must be completed. Review your schedule daily to remind yourself which tasks must be done that day.

▶ **Use technology.** Technology simplifies and expedites many tasks that previously required significant amounts of time to finish. Determine whether and how technology can help you complete your work more efficiently.

▶ **Use your scheduling tools.** Use a schedule to plan the work steps for tasks. Stick to the schedule, even if it means accomplishing something you do not enjoy. Once you have completed the "dreaded" task, congratulate yourself on a job well done. Celebrate and reward yourself for large accomplishments.

▶ **Stay organized.** Disorganization leads to procrastination. Consciously or unconsciously, people are likely to avoid disorganized and chaotic situations.

▶ **Make it fun.** Break up the monotony of working on a large project by completing tasks as creatively as possible. Of course, keep your creativity within professional boundaries and use it to produce work of high quality.

▶ **Avoid perfectionism.** Put forth your best effort. Strive for quality by giving your best performance, but recognize that it is acceptable to be imperfect.

▶ **Look for professional development opportunities.** Avoid thinking of the project as a chore but think of it as an opportunity and a challenge. Consider how you can grow professionally from the experience.

▌ **Seek assistance when necessary.** Ask for help when you need it rather than struggle on your own to figure out something that confuses you or that you lack the skills to understand or complete. Ask for clarification of anything you are unclear about.

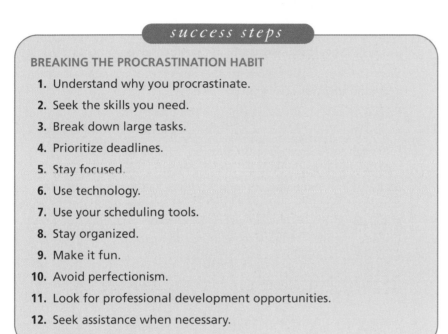

success steps

BREAKING THE PROCRASTINATION HABIT

1. Understand why you procrastinate.

2. Seek the skills you need.

3. Break down large tasks.

4. Prioritize deadlines.

5. Stay focused.

6. Use technology.

7. Use your scheduling tools.

8. Stay organized.

9. Make it fun.

10. Avoid perfectionism.

11. Look for professional development opportunities.

12. Seek assistance when necessary.

▌ REFLECTION QUESTION

• If you are a procrastinator, how will you eliminate this habit?

DELEGATING EFFECTIVELY

Depending on the task that needs to be accomplished, you may need to delegate certain responsibilities to efficiently complete a project. When a task is issued to an individual, it is that person's responsibility to determine whether completing the task requires assistance from others and, if so, to communicate this. Delegating is typically the responsibility of department managers or project managers. If delegating is done correctly, it can be a major factor in good time management.

Study these steps to effective delegating, which are based on work by Morgan (2000; updated 2004) and McNamara (1999):

Step 1. Recognize when delegation is appropriate.

Step 2. Believe in and trust the abilities of others. Recognize that although their work may be different from yours, their work can still be satisfactory.

Effective delegation can be a major factor in good time management.

Step 3. Make sure you completely understand what the task entails prior to delegating it. If you are clear on what must be accomplished, then you can more clearly relay that information to others.

Step 4. Write down what must be accomplished to complete the task and your expectations for completion. Make sure directions are clearly stated. Have someone read them over and provide you with feedback to ensure that the steps are clearly stated and correctly ordered. Provide this written material when delegating the work.

Step 5. Select project team members based on their skills, abilities, and time availability.

Step 6. When you head a project team, create an open environment for informal communication and inform team members that questions are welcome. Schedule periodic meetings to ensure effective communication among team members.

Step 7. Depending on how long a project will take to complete, schedule formal methods of reporting progress and submitting work at regular intervals. Review and evaluate work as it comes in. Provide ongoing feedback to team members.

Step 8. Be flexible and make adjustments as needed regarding individual responsibilities.

> ▶ REFLECTION QUESTIONS
>
> - How have you gone about delegating in the past?
> - How can you improve your delegating skills?

5

REDUCING E-MAIL OVERLOAD

Distractions take up valuable time in the workplace. Distractions come in various forms, including telephone calls, visits with coworkers, and e-mails. Conducting an evaluation of your use of time through an activity log is the first step in determining whether distractions are a problem.

The Internet and e-mail enhance and improve communication, but using them can become a significant distraction that greatly affects your productivity. However, you can take steps to ensure that these technologies remain tools and do not become distractions.

Study the following tips on utilizing e-mail effectively (Duncan, 2005b, c):

▶ **Organize your e-mail.** Organize your e-mails into subject categories. Create separate files for subject categories. As e-mails are received, save them as needed in the appropriate file for future reference. This method helps to alleviate overload in your inbox, allowing it to contain only the most recently received messages.

Utilizing this method means that you take spend less time checking your inbox throughout the day. Think of the inbox as a temporary rather than a permanent storage area. If you have to scroll through your inbox, then you are either not checking your e-mail frequently enough or you need to further organize your inbox for more effective use.

▶ **Reserve specific times to check e-mail.** When scheduling your work, reserve certain times throughout the day to check and respond to e-mails. Responding to e-mails as they arrive can become a distraction and affect your productivity. When you do respond to e-mails, do so promptly, as procrastination creates disorganization and a backlog of messages to be dealt with.

▶ **Be selective about printing e-mails.** Avoid printing every e-mail; doing so wastes time and creates paper clutter. Save e-mails as documentation in their appropriate folder and print only those for which you actually need a hard copy.

▶ **Keep e-mails professional.** Sending and receiving e-mails of jokes and pictures is not appropriate in the workplace. Spending time sending and reading junk mail is unproductive, can reduce your credibility, and uses a significant amount of time.

▶ **Use technology to your advantage.** Use other software applications, such as Microsoft Outlook™, to address e-mail management issues.

▶ **Use e-mail filters.** Similarly, take advantage of software that blocks "spam." (Most organizations incorporate these types of filters into their systems.) Eliminating spam increases productivity because it eliminates the need for employees to spend time sorting through junk mail and reduces the risk of harmful programs being introduced into companies' computer systems.

5

success steps

1. Organize your e-mail.
2. Reserve specific times to check e-mail.
3. Be selective about printing e-mails.
4. Keep e-mails professional.
5. Use technology to your advantage.
6. Use e-mail filters.

? CRITICAL THINKING QUESTION

5–2. What is your reaction to the following statement: "As long as I get the job done on time, issues regarding time management don't really concern me"?

5

TIME MANAGEMENT: SOME FINAL TIPS

The goal of effective time management is to be productive in both your personal and professional lives. You can accomplish a great deal by establishing wise time-use skills. There is no one solution to good time management, however: "Time management is a highly personalized skill, and whatever method works for you is the right one" (Idaho State University, n.d., p. 1). It is up to each of us to determine which time management tools work best for us.

CHAPTER SUMMARY

This chapter addressed major concepts related to time management. You were introduced to a process that includes determining goals and then using those goals to create a to do list of related tasks, as well as an action plan to complete each task and its objective. Next, you were introduced to scheduling steps that can help you prioritize tasks so that each can be completed in a timely manner. You learned that lower-priority tasks can be delayed and are likely to become higher priority as their deadlines draw near. Organizational strategies were emphasized as a means of using time wisely. Finally, you learned methods for addressing procrastination and concepts of delegating to maximize your time management efforts.

POINTS TO REMEMBER

In this chapter, several main points were discussed in detail:

- Learning strong time management skills can positively affect all aspects of your life.
- Using effective time management skills can make work more enjoyable and life in general more rewarding.
- Establishing goals that guide one in a successful career and help to balance all areas of one's life contributes to success.
- Set goals in a variety of areas in your life.
- Writing an action plan defines tasks more effectively and allows progress to be more easily monitored.
- Using planning aids, such as planning books, electronic planners, computer software programs, and to do lists, helps you organize your time.

▶ Using time unwisely results in uncompleted tasks and unmet deadlines, regardless of how much goal setting and planning is done.

▶ Keeping an activity log for a week or so can help you analyze where your time is wisely used, where it is wasted, and when you are at peak performance.

▶ Being disorganized in your personal life can greatly impact your professional success.

▶ Scheduling your time wisely enables you to accomplish tasks in a timely manner with less stress.

▶ Overcoming procrastination requires that you understand why you procrastinate and then learn how to break the habitual cycle.

▶ Delegating tasks when necessary is a key to good time management if the delegating is done correctly.

▶ Using e-mail enhances and improves communication, but if misused, it wastes valuable time.

LEARNING OBJECTIVES REVISITED

Review the learning objectives for this chapter and rate your level of achievement for each objective using the rating scale provided. For each objective on which you do not rate yourself as a 3, outline a plan of action that you will take to fully achieve the objective. Include a time frame for this plan.

1 = did not successfully achieve objective

2 = understand what is needed, but need more study or practice

3 = achieved learning objective thoroughly

	1	2	3
Identify steps to scheduling.	☐	☐	☐
Appreciate the importance of developing effective time management skills.	☐	☐	☐
Explain how to set effective goals.	☐	☐	☐
Describe methods to become more organized.	☐	☐	☐
Discuss various types of planning aids and scheduling tools that can be utilized in the workplace.	☐	☐	☐
Explain how to break the habit of procrastination.	☐	☐	☐
Describe the steps to effective delegation.	☐	☐	☐
Discuss how to utilize e-mail effectively.	☐	☐	☐

	1	2	3
Analyze your use of time and draw conclusions from this analysis.	☐	☐	☐
Demonstrate the ability to create a to do list and prioritize each task.	☐	☐	☐

Steps to Achieve Unmet Objectives

Steps   Due Date

1. _____   _____

2. _____   _____

3. _____   _____

4. _____   _____

SUGGESTED ITEMS FOR LEARNING PORTFOLIO

Refer to the "Developing Portfolios" section at the front of this textbook for more information on learning portfolios.

▶ Analyzing Time: This activity will give you insight into how you use your time.

▶ Create a To Do List and Action Plan: This activity will provide you with experience in prioritizing your tasks.

▶ Research and Presentation: The goal of this activity is to familiarize you with types of time management tools.

REFERENCES

Duncan, P. (2005a). Sweating right up to the last minute: Battling procrastination [electronic version]. Retrieved April 21, 2005, from http://stress.about.com/cs/timemanagement/a/aa112002.htm

Duncan, P. (2005b). Reducing e-mail overload and the stress that comes with it [electronic version]. Retrieved April 21, 2005, from http://stress.about.com/od/timemanagement/a/emailstress.htm

Duncan, P. (2005c). Three guaranteed ways to reduce e-mail overload and the stress it causes [electronic version]. Retrieved April 21, 2005, from http://stress.about.com/od/timemanagement/a/emailstress_2.htm

Idaho State University. (n.d.). Effective time management [electronic version]. *Lead to Succeed Leadership Education and Training Resource Information Series.* Retrieved April 21, 2005, from http://www.isu.edu/stdorg/lead/resource/time.html

Janssen, D. A. (n.d.). The ultimate self-challenge: Time management [electronic version]. Welcome to danieljanssen.com, A division of Practical Planning Publishing. Retrieved April 21, 2005, from http://www.danieljanssen.com/ArchiveArticles/timemanagement.shtml

McNamara, C. (1999). Basics of delegating [electronic version]. Retrieved April 21, 2005, from http://www.mapnp.org/library/guiding/delegating/basics.htm

Mind Tools. (1995–2006). Personal goal setting: Find direction—live life your way. Retrieved July 21, 2006 from http://www.mindtools.com/page6.html

Mind Tools (1995–2005a). To-Do lists—remembering to do all essential tasks in the right order [electronic version]. Retrieved April 21, 2005, from http://www.mindtools.com/pages/article/newHTE_05.htm

Mind Tools. (1995–2005b). Action plans—small scale planning [electronic version]. Retrieved April 21, 2005, from http://www.mindtools.com/pages/article/newHTE_04.htm

Mind Tools. (1995–2005c). Activity logs—finding out how you really spend your time [electronic version]. Retrieved April 21, 2005, from http://www.mindtools.com/pages/article/newHTE_03.htm

Mind Tools. (1995–2005d). Effective scheduling—planning to make the best use of your time [electronic version]. Retrieved April 21, 2005, from http://www.mindtools.com/pages/article/newHTE_07.htm

Morgan, R. L. (2000) (Updated 2004). 12 tips for delegating effectively [electronic version]. Retrieved April 21, 2005, from http://www.ivillage.co.uk/workcareer/survive/prodskills/articles/0,156890,00.html

Pavlina, S. (2001). Overcoming procrastination [electronic version]. Retrieved April 21, 2005, from http://www.dexterity.com/articles/overcoming-procrastination.htm

Quek, T. (2002). The problem of procrastination [electronic version]. Retrieved April 21, 2005, from http://webhome.idirect.com/~readon/procrat.html

Tufts College. (2002). Organizational development and training tip sheet . . . time management [electronic version]. Tufts University. Retrieved April 21, 2005, from http://www.tufts.edu/hr/tips/time.html

©Image 100 Ltd.

CHAPTER OUTLINE

6 Project Management

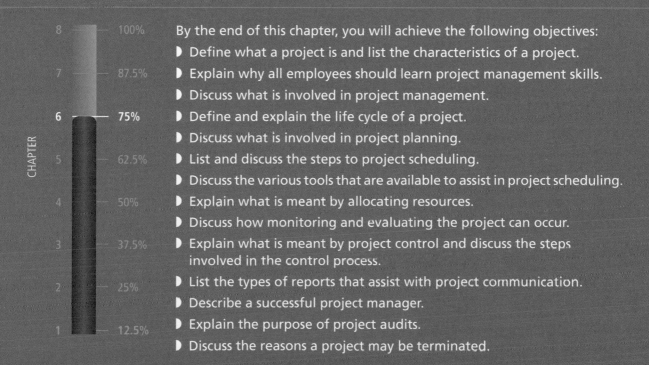

THE BIG PICTURE

CHAPTER		
8		100%
7		87.5%
6		**75%**
5		62.5%
4		50%
3		37.5%
2		25%
1		12.5%

LEARNING OBJECTIVES

By the end of this chapter, you will achieve the following objectives:

▶ Define what a project is and list the characteristics of a project.

▶ Explain why all employees should learn project management skills.

▶ Discuss what is involved in project management.

▶ Define and explain the life cycle of a project.

▶ Discuss what is involved in project planning.

▶ List and discuss the steps to project scheduling.

▶ Discuss the various tools that are available to assist in project scheduling.

▶ Explain what is meant by allocating resources.

▶ Discuss how monitoring and evaluating the project can occur.

▶ Explain what is meant by project control and discuss the steps involved in the control process.

▶ List the types of reports that assist with project communication.

▶ Describe a successful project manager.

▶ Explain the purpose of project audits.

▶ Discuss the reasons a project may be terminated.

6

TOPIC SCENARIO

Janice has just been placed in charge of two projects at her place of employment. One project is quite small and is predicted to take about two months to complete. The other project is projected to last about two years.

Based on this scenario, answer the following questions:

▶ Now that Janice has been given these projects, what steps should she take?

▶ What tools might help Janice develop a clearer understanding of these projects?

▶ What are the similarities and differences between these projects?

▶ What management skills will Janice need as a project leader?

PROJECT MANAGEMENT: AN OVERVIEW

This chapter introduces project management and the tools and skills necessary for successful project completion. A project can be defined as "a one-time set of activities that ends with a specific accomplishment." A project is characterized as follows (Chapman, 2004):

▶ Tasks are nonroutine.

▶ Tasks lead to a specific goal.

▶ There are definite start and finish dates.

▶ There are designated and limited resources.

Managers are not the only employees who manage projects. Most employees have tasks or projects that must be completed on time, within the stated perimeters of the task, and within a budget. Consequently, any employee tasked with the responsibility of completing a project can benefit from learning effective project management skills.

Project management encompasses many tasks, including defining the tasks that will result in the finished project, planning and scheduling the tasks to be completed by the defined deadline, and controlling task completion to reach the goal within the allocation of the resources (Lowery, 1994, p. 2). A successful project manager meets the requirements and goals of the project on time and within budget.

Projects come in many sizes. Some projects may be small tasks to be completed by one person or larger tasks that require a project manager to work with a group of individuals. The larger the scope of the project, the more complex it becomes. The project manager is the individual who is in charge of seeing the project to a successful end. Study the following components critical to reaching a project goal.

▶ **Organization.** Organization consists primarily of setting goals and identifying tasks and the action plans to complete them. Identify the resources needed for carrying out each action plan. Organize and coordinate several elements of the task, such as the various steps and any supplies you will need, to ensure a successful outcome.

▶ **Planning.** Planning includes determining the human and material resources required to support the project objectives and goals, as well as defining strategies for the efficient use of those resources. Devise schedules to ensure that the project is completed on time and unexpected events are taken into consideration. All planning must be done with the goal of staying within the designated budget.

▶ **Gathering information resources.** In addition to human and material resources, it is necessary to obtain information necessary for the completion of the project. For example, the project manager and team must know client needs and expectations, vendor schedules, and general information regarding procedures and strategies.

▶ **Leadership.** Project teams must work collaboratively as well remain focused and on schedule. It is the project manager's job to provide the leadership that maintains positive group dynamics and a cohesive project team.

▶ **Evaluation.** To remain on track, progress toward project goals must be evaluated regularly. If necessary, resources and schedules can be revised and processes modified to keep the project moving toward its goals.

▶ **Communication.** A consistent flow of information among all stakeholders in the project is essential. In addition to ensuring that effective communication occurs among team members, it is important to keep the client informed and happy with the project's progress. Senior management must also be kept informed of the project status.

THE LIFE CYCLE OF A PROJECT

The life cycle of a project is defined as "the phases that a project goes through from concept through completion" (Lewis, 1995, p. 340). Regardless of the size of a project, the key to success is to follow some basic project management techniques to plan, organize, motivate, direct, and control the project through the various phases of the life cycle of the project. Author David Cleland (1994, p. 47) defines four phases of project planning and the tasks typically associated with each, as illustrated in Figure 6–1.

▶ REFLECTION QUESTIONS

- What projects in your personal and/or professional life have you been in charge of?
- Were you successful? If so, why? If not, why not?
- What areas might you be able to improve?

? CRITICAL THINKING QUESTIONS

6–1. What would the difference be in managing a large project versus a small project?

6–2. What challenges might you experience with each type?

Phase 1: Conceptual	Phase 2: Planning	Phase 3: Execution	Phase 4: Termination
Identify need	Implement schedule	Procure materials	Train functional personnel
Establish feasibility	Conduct studies and analyses	Build and test tooling	Transfer materials
Identify alternatives	Design systems	Develop support requirements	Transfer responsibility
Prepare proposal	Build and test prototypes	Produce system	Release resources
Develop basic team budget and schedule	Analyze results	Verify performance	Reassign project members
Identify project team	Obtain approval for production	Modify as required	

FIGURE 6–1. A summary of the tasks of each of the project management phases.

PROJECT PLANNING

Project planning is a significant factor in project management and is the guide for the project team's progress. Although time-consuming to create, the project plan is crucial to a project's success. For large projects, technical tools such as a Gantt chart (a graph that tracks the relationships of project components, schedules, and progress) may be useful. Smaller projects need less complex tools but still require some type of time management planning. Planning a project begins with focusing on time management, which is a critical element of successful project completion. To determine the amount of time a project will take to finish, it is important to consider the project as a whole and to understand its full scope. Planning involves understanding what the project will look like when it is completed and creating a detailed list of the tasks that are required for completion. Study the following questions, which should be considered during the planning phase (Lewis, 1995).

▶ What must be done?
▶ How should it be done?
▶ Who should do it?
▶ When must it be done?
▶ How much will it cost?

Planning the duration of a project includes determining how much time is required for project tasks, such as meetings, emergencies, sicknesses, and holidays; equipment requirements; delivery problems; and staffing issues (Mind Tools, 1995–2005a). Allocating sufficient and accurate amounts of time for individual tasks results in a project delivered in a timely manner. Nonetheless, planners frequently lack a realistic sense of what is involved in a project and thus underestimate the time needed to complete the various tasks that compose the project. The consequences of inaccurately estimating a project's timeline include delays that create problems with deadlines and project delivery, increased stress among team members, and potential financial and credibility losses.

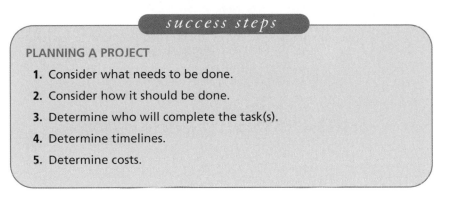

success steps

PLANNING A PROJECT

1. Consider what needs to be done.
2. Consider how it should be done.
3. Determine who will complete the task(s).
4. Determine timelines.
5. Determine costs.

Another common mistake made by project planners is not involving the project team in the planning process. If the project manager makes all decisions unilaterally, the decisions may be self-referenced and not reflective of the realities of the project (Lewis, 1995).

One way to involve team members (and achieve a timely outcome) is to establish a breakdown of short-term project objectives as part of the planning process. Particularly for large projects, set goals and objectives that can be measured throughout the life of the project. Doing this creates a method of measuring progress, which, in turn, gives the project team members opportunities to feel a sense of satisfaction and completion during the various stages of the project.

ANALYSIS

Project planning typically includes a SWOT analysis, which analyzes the **S**trengths, **W**eaknesses, **O**pportunities, and **T**hreats that may affect the project. A risk analysis that determines what could go wrong during the project can also be conducted. When doing any type of project risk analysis, however, take care not to try to identify *all* possible risks, as doing so can impede progress on the project (Lewis, 1995).

THE WORK BREAKDOWN STRUCTURE

Project planning for larger projects requires the work to be broken down into various goals, or work packages, and then later distributed to the

Completing a project as a team requires strong collaborative and communication skills.

appropriate individual(s) for "assembly" and completion. The easiest way to complete a work breakdown structure (WBS) is to determine what must be accomplished in order to complete the project. In project management, developing the WBS is one of the most important steps because it "provides a framework" for the following (Lewis, 1995):

▶ identifies all allocated tasks and resources

▶ allows estimations of task durations based on resource allocations

▶ allows incorporation of costs and resource allocations into the overall project budget

▶ provides a basis for developing a working schedule for the project

▶ provides a basis for tracking performance against identified costs, schedules, and resource allocations

▶ allows responsibility to be assigned for each task element

Figure 6–2 provides an example of a simple WBS for the planning of a banquet (Chapman, 1997, updated 2004, p. 1).

The number of levels in a WBS is dependent on the size of the project. Often, a six-level WBS is sufficient. Lewis (1995) suggests no more than 20 levels be used, regardless of the size of the project.

Once the project plan is done, depending on the type and size of the project, a written plan of the project may be required. In addition, the plan may need to be signed off by upper management and other directors.

▶ REFLECTION QUESTIONS

• Are you a good planner?
• When planning, do you normally think of everything or do you have a tendency to lack detail in your planning?
• If this is area that needs work, what will you do to improve?

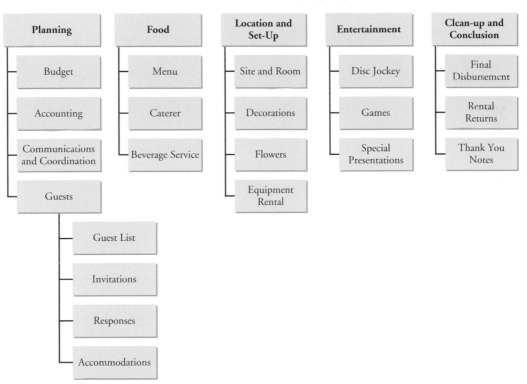

The Work Breakdown Structure (WBS)

FIGURE 6–2. This example of a WBS is based on planning a party. Major tasks are designated by category so that responsibility can be assigned accordingly. Notice how tasks can be broken down further to define additional detail, as illustrated by "Guests."

6

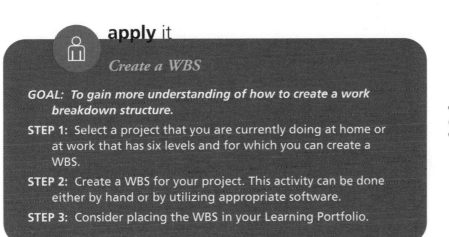

apply it

Create a WBS

GOAL: To gain more understanding of how to create a work breakdown structure.

STEP 1: Select a project that you are currently doing at home or at work that has six levels and for which you can create a WBS.

STEP 2: Create a WBS for your project. This activity can be done either by hand or by utilizing appropriate software.

STEP 3: Consider placing the WBS in your Learning Portfolio.

? CRITICAL THINKING QUESTION

6–3. What is your reaction to the following statement: "To be a good project manager, an individual will need more skills than just project planning"? Explain your answer.

PROJECT SCHEDULING

The size of the project partially determines how simple or complex the project schedule will be. Smaller projects composed of relatively simple tasks that involve only one or two people take less coordination, naturally, than large projects requiring the coordination of multiple project elements and complex tasks that involve many employees. The basic steps of scheduling are as follows (Lowery, 1994):

1. Specify what needs to be done by defining tasks and contingencies.

2. Schedule when the tasks must be completed.

3. Determine how each task must be accomplished by assigning people, equipment, and funding.

Various project scheduling tools are available. For complex projects, tools such as Gantt charts, Critical Path Analysis (CPA), and PERT charts (Program Evaluation and Review Technique) are helpful in both planning and monitoring projects. For example, Gantt charts "allow you to assess how long a project should take, determine the resources needed, and lay out the order in which tasks need to be carried out" (Mind Tools, 1995–2005b, p. 4). Microsoft Project™ is an example of software that can generate Gantt charts.

Employees, including project managers, may need to be trained to use these tools so that the tools can be used to manage large projects efficiently. For smaller projects, simple flowcharts can be effective. Generally, the benefits of using scheduling software outweigh any difficulty involved with learning how to use it. Consider the following benefits to using project management software (Lowery, 1994):

▶ The project schedule can be created and revised quickly.

▶ The schedule resources are easily analyzed.

▶ Alternative solutions to scheduling problems can be readily determined.

▶ One scheduling tool allows centralized planning throughout the organization.

▶ Output in a standard format is easy to produce, accurate, and consistent for all projects.

▶ Information can be tailored as appropriate for all stakeholders, making timely and valid information available as it is needed.

▶ Progress, schedule, resources, and costs are more easily tracked and controlled.

Successful development of a project master schedule is dependent on some basic steps that should be executed in sequential order. These steps are listed below (Cleland, 1994, p. 253).

Step 1. Define project objectives, goals, and general strategies.

Step 2. Develop the work breakdown structure (WBS).

Step 3. Sequence the project tasks.

Step 4. Estimate the time frame and cost of each task.

Step 5. Review the master schedule noting contingencies and time constraints.

Step 6. Consider and reconcile schedule and costs with available resources.

Step 7. Ensure that the schedule supports cost constraints and allows for effective completion of project components.

Step 8. Obtain management approval as required.

---

success steps

DEVELOPING A PROJECT SCHEDULE

1. Define objectives and goals.

2. Develop the work breakdown structure (WBS).

3. Sequence tasks.

4. Estimate time and cost of each task.

5. Compare to master schedule.

6. Reconcile any schedule and cost discrepancies.

7. Ensure schedule is compatible with goals.

8. Get final approval.

6

When planning a project, it is critical to keep in mind that some activities are dependent on other activities being completed first. Dependent activities need to be completed in a sequence, with tasks providing the foundation for the next stage being completed first or completed to a stage that supports the next step. These activities are known as sequential activities. Activities that are not dependent on other tasks and can be done at any time are called parallel tasks (Mind Tools, 1995–2005b).

apply it

Scheduling Tools

GOAL: **To better understand Gantt charts, Critical Path Analysis (CPA), and PERT (Program Evaluation and Review Technique) charts.**

STEP 1: Divide the class into groups of four.

STEP 2: Select a scheduling tool for each group to research, ensuring that each group has a different tool. Each group should present an explanation of its scheduling tool to the other groups. If possible, each group should devise a sample schedule using the tool it researched.

STEP 3: Consider putting this information in your Learning Portfolio.

ALLOCATING RESOURCES

Allocating resources includes assigning human and material resources to each task making up the project. Charting the distribution of resources is critical to determining whether enough resources will be available through the project. A project will fail if adequate resources are not available for its duration.

As with scheduling, resource allocation can be done using a variety of charts and graphs. For example, Microsoft Project™ includes a Resource

Project management software can facilitate the project management process.

Name Form that allows project managers to enter information regarding various resources that will be utilized for projects. Once the information is entered, the managers can then use the Resource Graph to monitor allocation of the resources and costs for both the project and individual tasks (Lowery, 1994). Resources should be monitored and adjusted as needed on an ongoing basis until project completion.

PROJECT CONTROL

Monitoring and controlling a project are the tasks of the project manager. Monitoring the project means working with the project team to ensure that the work is being accomplished according to the project's requirements and that the established deadlines are being met. Monitoring and evaluating should occur throughout the life cycle of a project, utilizing informal and formal methods.

Controlling a project effectively refers to monitoring the progress of the *project,* not monitoring and controlling the team members. Controlling and micromanaging team members can cause resentment as well as constrain creativity and the team collaboration that is vital to the success of a project (Lewis, 1995).

REFLECTION QUESTIONS

- How comfortable are you with computers?
- Do you think your knowledge regarding computers is sufficient for your profession?
- If not, what plans do you need to make to increase your knowledge and abilities?

CRITICAL THINKING QUESTION

6–4. Regardless of the size of a project, can successful scheduling be done without using computers? Explain your answer.

6

©Digital Vision

The person in charge of a project has significant responsibility for and influence over the outcome of a project.

To empower project team members, project managers must supply each team member with the following information (Lewis, 1995).

▶ A clear definition of the expectations and purpose associated with the assigned tasks.

▶ A plan on outlining requirements of the tasks.

▶ A description of the skills needed to complete the task.

▶ Adequate resources to do the work.

▶ Feedback on progress throughout the task.

▶ A clear definition of her authority to correct variations in the original plan. All team members should have the necessary authority to be able to respond to issues that arise.

The term *project control* indicates the process whereby the project manager monitors, evaluates, and compares expected goals with the actual progress that has been accomplished (Cleland, 1994). By reviewing these areas, the project manager can determine where control is lacking and what kinds of changes needed to be implemented.

The control process can be viewed as a cycle of distinct steps (Cleland, 1994).

Step 1. Establish performance standards for the project.

Step 2. Observe performance through both formal and informal methods.

Step 3. Compare actual performance with planned performance.

Step 4. Take corrective action where necessary.

success steps

CONTROLLING THE PROJECT PROCESS

1. Establish standards for the project.

2. Observe performance.

3. Compare performance to standards.

4. Make corrections and adjustments as needed.

By conducting evaluations, project managers can stay in control of projects and make adjustments when needed. Project managers should make the following considerations during the control cycle (Cleland, 1994, p. 289).

▶ Status of the project and project work packages in terms of schedule, cost, performance, objectives, and goals.

▶ Successful and unsuccessful aspects of the project.

▶ Problems and opportunities that become apparent as the project progresses.

▶ Additional actions that can be taken to improve the project.

▶ Effectiveness of the project team.

PROJECT COMMUNICATION AND LEADERSHIP

Communication among everyone involved with a project throughout its duration is critical to its success. Effective communication must occur among a variety of individuals, including project team members, management, customers, and stakeholders. Communication should occur informally and formally. Project schedules should include formal meetings to update individuals about the project's progress. The frequency of these meetings may change depending on issues that arise. If more meetings are required, then the schedule must be adjusted to accommodate them.

Reports are useful for communicating information to team members and stakeholders in the project. Below is a list of various report types commonly used in the communication process (Lowery, 1994).

▶ Summary reports indicate progress on individual tasks.

▶ Exception reports indicate discrepancies with the original schedule.

▶ Solution reports suggest possible resolutions to problems and show schedule revisions based on proposed changes. These reports provide the foundation for decisions about the exceptions.

▶ Direction reports provide the supervisors of individual tasks with information regarding updates as well as objectives and resources for the next phase of the project.

THE CHARACTERISTICS OF SUCCESSFUL PROJECT MANAGERS

The success of a project is largely dependent on the individual in charge of the project and the ability of that individual to both manage the success of the project and lead team members in accomplishing the required objectives (Cleland, 1994). The project leader is responsible for providing a vision of the project to the project team members and for encouraging and motivating their success.

▶ REFLECTION QUESTIONS

• How might you perform as a project manager?
• Do you think team members would enjoy working with you? Why, or why not?

? CRITICAL THINKING QUESTION

6–5. What is your reaction to this statement: "On a project, there are always some team members who need to be controlled"?

6

Consider the following characteristics of a successful project manager:

- ability to plan and organize the project resources
- ability to identify and solve problems
- team-building skills
- ability to see the "big picture"
- financial acumen
- ability to communicate and resolve conflict
- negotiation skills
- creativity and innovation skills

success steps

DEVELOPING PROJECT MANAGER SKILLS

1. Develop planning and organizational skills.
2. Be able to identify and solve problems.
3. Know how to build a team.
4. See the "big picture."
5. Develop your financial acumen.
6. Develop excellent communication and conflict resolution skills.
7. Be able to negotiate.
8. Develop your creativity and innovation.

6

▶ REFLECTION QUESTIONS

- What leadership qualities do you have to offer?
- What leadership qualities might you need to develop?

? CRITICAL THINKING QUESTION

6–6. What do you look for in a good leader?

©Image 100 Ltd.

Regular reports of a project's progress keep project team members informed and on track.

PROJECT TERMINATION

Everyone hopes that his or her projects are successful and that the goals of the project are met. Unfortunately, some projects are terminated due to failure. Projects may fail due to financial reasons, schedule failures, technical issues, or changes in the organization that render the project incompatible with altered long-term plans (Cleland, 1994).

Project audits, which are normally completed by individuals not involved with the project, can determine the cause of a project's failure and pinpoint the stage or stages at which critical breakdowns occurred. Uninvolved individuals are more likely to be objective in their evaluation of the project's viability and effectiveness (Cleland, 1994). Project team members should consider audits as a learning process intended to improve performance, rather than as being punitive (Lewis, 1995).

Project audits should (Cleland, 1994, p. 295)

▶ Determine what is effective and ineffective, and why.

▶ Identify elements that have adversely affected the achievement of cost, schedule, and technical performance objectives.

▶ Evaluate the current project management strategy, including organizational support, policies, procedures, practices, techniques, guidelines, action plans, funding, and resources utilization.

▶ Provide an opportunity for team members to exchange ideas and information, and identify problems that affected the project, as well as potential solutions and strategies.

Termination of a project is typically not taken lightly, and involvement of other individuals within the organization in this decision may be required. Termination may be a solution to one or more of the following issues (Cleland, 1994):

▶ The project is severely behind schedule and over budget.

▶ Technical performance is compromised, or technical risks are too great.

▶ The project does not fit with the sponsoring organization's strategic plan.

▶ The customer's plans have changed.

▶ Competition has changed in a way that makes or threatens to make project outcomes obsolete.

▶ Organizational goals have changed in a way that contradicts the original purpose of the project.

Regardless of whether a project has been determined to be a success or a failure, a post-project review (PPR) should be conducted. "PPRs offer insight

6

into the success or failure of a particular project as well as a composite of lessons learned from a review of all the projects in the organization's portfolio or capital projects" (Cleland, 1994). Organizations can and should learn from project successes and failures.

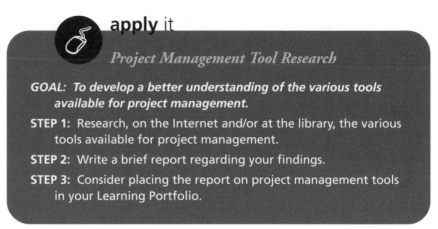

apply it

Project Management Tool Research

GOAL: *To develop a better understanding of the various tools available for project management.*

STEP 1: Research, on the Internet and/or at the library, the various tools available for project management.

STEP 2: Write a brief report regarding your findings.

STEP 3: Consider placing the report on project management tools in your Learning Portfolio.

CHAPTER SUMMARY

This chapter explored project management as a tool for professionals, both in the formal role as a project manager and for individuals who can use the concepts of project management to manage daily assignments. You learned the elements of successful project management, including planning, scheduling, controlling, and evaluating. You were introduced to several project management tools, including work breakdown structures (WBSs), Gantt charts, Critical Path Analyses (CPAs), and PERT (Program Evaluation and Review Technique) charts. In addition, you became acquainted with reports that are typically provided to project team members and other stakeholders involved in the project. Finally, termination of projects was reviewed, and the characteristics of both successful and unsuccessful projects were summarized.

POINTS TO KEEP IN MIND

In this chapter, several main points were discussed in detail:

 ▌ Any employee tasked with the responsibility of completing a project can benefit from learning effective project management skills.

▶ The project manager is the individual who is in charge of seeing a project to a successful end.

▶ The key to project success, regardless of the project's size, is following basic project management techniques to plan, organize, motivate, direct, and control the project through the various phases of its life cycle.

▶ Project planning can be time-consuming, but neglecting this task usually results in project failure.

▶ To accurately determine the amount of time a certain project will take, it is important to look at the project as a whole and to understand its full scope.

▶ Effective project planning involves understanding what the project will look like when it is completed and creating a detailed list of the tasks that are required for completion.

▶ Time-estimate errors are more likely to occur when team members are not included in the planning process.

▶ The establishment of goals and objectives is important to the successful analysis of a project's outcome.

▶ During project planning, a SWOT and a risk analysis should be conducted and a WBS should be developed.

▶ The number of levels in a WBS depends on the size of the project. Often, a six-level WBS is sufficient.

▶ Various tools are available for project scheduling, including Gantt charts, Critical Path Analysis (CPA), and PERT (Program Evaluation and Review Technique) charts.

▶ A project will fail if an inadequate amount of resources is available to support it. Charting resources is critical to determining whether enough will be available throughout the project.

▶ Project monitoring and evaluating should occur throughout a project and utilize both formal and informal methods.

▶ Effective managers must learn how to empower project team members.

▶ Project managers can stay in control of projects and make adjustments where needed by conducting evaluations.

▶ Communication among everyone involved with a project throughout its duration is critical to its success.

▶ The project leader is responsible for providing a vision of the project to the project team members and for encouraging and motivating their success.

▶ A project is successful if its goals have been met.

LEARNING OBJECTIVES REVISITED

Review the learning objectives for this chapter and rate your level of achievement for each objective using the rating scale provided. For each objective on which you do not rate yourself as a 3, outline a plan of action that you will take to fully achieve the objective. Include a time frame for this plan.

1 = did not successfully achieve objective

2 = understand what is needed, but need more study or practice

3 = achieved learning objective thoroughly

	1	2	3
Define what a project is and list the characteristics of a project.	☐	☐	☐
Explain why all employees should learn project management skills.	☐	☐	☐
Discuss what is involved in project management.	☐	☐	☐
Define and explain the life cycle of a project.	☐	☐	☐
Discuss what is involved in project planning.	☐	☐	☐
Explain why it is important to involve project team members in the planning process.	☐	☐	☐
Define and explain what is in entailed in a SWOT and risk analysis.	☐	☐	☐
Define WBS and explain its purpose.	☐	☐	☐
List and discuss the steps to project scheduling.	☐	☐	☐
Discuss the various tools that are available to assist in project scheduling.	☐	☐	☐
Describe the purpose of a Gantt chart and explain the steps to developing one.	☐	☐	☐
Explain what is meant by allocating resources.	☐	☐	☐
Discuss how monitoring and evaluating the project can occur.	☐	☐	☐
Describe the type of information that can help to empower project team members.	☐	☐	☐
Explain what is meant by project control and discuss the steps involved in the control process.	☐	☐	☐
Summarize the types of reports available to assist with project communication.	☐	☐	☐
Describe a successful project manager.	☐	☐	☐
Explain the purpose of a project audits.	☐	☐	☐
Discuss the reasons why a project may be terminated.	☐	☐	☐

6

Steps to Achieve Unmet Objectives

Steps	Due Date
1. _____	_____
2. _____	_____
3. _____	_____
4. _____	_____

SUGGESTED ITEMS FOR LEARNING PORTFOLIO

Refer to the "Developing Portfolios" section at the front of this textbook for more information on learning portfolios.

▶ Work Breakdown Structure: Completing this activity will provide you with experience in creating a work breakdown structure.

▶ Scheduling Tools: This activity will familiarize you with scheduling tools commonly used in the project management process.

▶ Project Management Tools: Complete this activity to learn more about project management tolls of your choice.

REFERENCES

Chapman, J. R. (1997, updated 2004). Work breakdown structure (WBS). Retrieved on May 5, 2005, from http://www.hyperthot.com/pm_wbs.htm

Cleland, D. I. (1994). *Project Management: Strategic Design and Implementation* (2nd ed.). New York: McGraw-Hill.

Lewis, J. P. (1995). *Project Planning, Scheduling & Control* (2nd ed.). Chicago: Irwin Professional Publishing.

Lowery, G. (1994). *Managing Projects with Microsoft Project 4.0: For Windows and Macintosh Version.* New York: Van Nostrand Reinhold.

Mind Tools. (1995–2005a). Estimating time accurately [electronic version]. Retrieved May 3, 2005, from http://www.mindtools.com/pages/article/newPPM_01.htm

Mind Tools. (1995–2005b). Gantt charts—planning and scheduling more complex projects [electronic version]. Retrieved May 3, 2005, from http://www.mindtools.com/pages/article/newPPM_03.htm

6

©Digital Vision

CHAPTER OUTLINE

The Office of the Twenty-First Century

Making a Positive First Impression

Dealing with Difficult People in the Workplace

Performance Appraisals, Raises, and Promotions

Workplace Etiquette Do's and Don'ts

7 Professionalism in the Workplace

THE BIG PICTURE

8	100%
7	**87.5%**
6	75%
5	62.5%
4	50%
3	37.5%
2	25%
1	12.5%

LEARNING OBJECTIVES

By the end of this chapter, you will achieve the following objectives:

▶ List qualities that employers seek when hiring new employees.
▶ List problem personality types and behaviors that can be encountered in the workplace.
▶ List and explain the steps involved when dealing with difficult people.
▶ Discuss the pros and cons of telecommuting.
▶ Explain how to make a good first impression at a new job.
▶ Understand methods for remaining positive and overcoming negativity.
▶ Explain methods of coping with a bad or ineffective supervisor.
▶ Discuss how to resolve workplace conflict.
▶ Understand the effects of stress and discuss how stress can be addressed proactively.
▶ Describe the purpose of performance appraisals.
▶ Explain the do's and don'ts of requesting a raise and obtaining a promotion.
▶ Discuss positive and negative office behavior.
▶ Discuss the issues that should be considered when attending a business lunch meeting or a company party.

7

TOPIC SCENARIO

Susan started work at her current employment a little over a year ago. During this time, she has received a lot of praise regarding her work from both her coworkers and her supervisor. Her performance appraisal, which occurred three months ago, confirmed that her work is outstanding. Two months ago, a new supervisor took over Susan's department and recently announced that all employees would receive new performance evaluations based on his observations of the last two months. Susan just walked out of her meeting with her supervisor and is astounded by what he has told her. Rather than receiving high marks, Susan has now been rated as a marginal employee.

Based on this short description of Susan's situation, answer the following questions:

- What should Susan's reaction be?
- Regardless of Susan's reaction, must she deal constructively and professionally with the situation?
- What wrong conclusions might Susan be making about the new supervisor?

THE OFFICE OF THE TWENTY-FIRST CENTURY

How and where work is accomplished has changed dramatically as technology has advanced. Some of the options available to employees include flex time, compressed work schedules, job sharing, and telecommuting.

Each of these situations has its own issues, but there is general agreement in the business world that employers benefit by offering these options, because doing so boosts loyalty, strengthens morale, minimizes turnover, and reduces recruitment and training expenses, as well as costs due to low productivity (Hansen, n.d.[a]).

Telecommuting in particular has become a more viable and popular option for employment. The number of employees working at home grew from 41.3 million in 2003 to 44.4 million in 2004, indicating an increase of 7.5% (Hansen, n.d.[d]).

Some employers resist instituting telecommuting for a variety of reasons, including being unable to meet with individuals as needed and the traditional perception that employees must be on site to function productively. However, with further development of technologies that make telecommuting more efficient and effective, more companies are finding this to be a viable work option for their employees (Greenspan, 2002). Greenspan cites technology such as broadband connections, more powerful computers, Web-conferencing capabilities, and Internet-based tools as devices that contribute to effective telecommuting.

Successful telecommuting depends on a variety of factors. Employees who do well in a telecommuting circumstance are those who are self-disciplined, self-motivated, well-organized, and proficient at time management. Evaluating your organizational skills and work style is important before you propose telecommuting to an employer (Hansen, n.d.[b]). In addition, prior to beginning employment with a company, it is important that you and your prospective employer address how and where work will be performed. Even if telecommuting is not presently an option, proposing it at a later time may be appropriate.

apply it

Telecommuting Opportunities

GOAL: To develop understanding about what is involved in telecommuting and whether it is feasible in your profession.

STEP 1: Conduct research on the Internet and/or at the library to find out more about telecommuting in your chosen profession.

STEP 2: Write a brief report of your findings and be prepared to present it to the class.

STEP 3: Consider placing the report on telecommuting opportunities in your Learning Portfolio.

MAKING A POSITIVE FIRST IMPRESSION

Whether you are telecommuting or working on site, making a good first impression is important for overall job success and for establishing positive relationships with both your supervisor and coworkers. Consider the following qualities and skills as those most highly valued by employers when hiring a new employee (Marquette University Career Services Center, 2003–2004):

- Communication skills (verbal, written, and presentation)
- Honesty and integrity
- The ability to relate well to others
- Showing motivation, initiative, and self-direction
- A strong work ethic

REFLECTION QUESTION

- Do you think you would be a good candidate for telecommuting? Explain your answer.

CRITICAL THINKING QUESTION

7–1. What is your response to the following statement: "It takes a lot of trust from an employer to allow an individual to telecommute"?

7

©2005 Jupiterimages Corporation

The professional image you project, including your appearance, contributes significantly to the impressions you make at your interview and in the first days of your job.

▶ Teamwork skills and the ability to work collaboratively

▶ Analytical and critical thinking skills

▶ Flexibility and adaptability to change

▶ Ability to attend to details

▶ Organization skills

▶ Self-confidence

▶ An appropriately friendly and outgoing personality

▶ The ability to communicate with tact and respect

▶ Good manners and courtesy

▶ Creativity

▶ A sense of humor

In the early days of your employment at a new job, it is important to demonstrate these qualities and abilities in order to make positive first impressions. Coworkers and supervisors want to know that the individual they have hired and are working with has the skills and qualities needed to get along with others and accomplish the required tasks.

When first starting a job, the following behaviors are significant in making a good first impression (Hansen & Hansen, n.d.):

▶ Having a positive attitude and demonstrating enthusiasm about the job

▶ Dressing professionally

▶ Showing team spirit by demonstrating a willingness to cooperate and collaborate with coworkers

▶ Giving credit to team members as appropriate

▶ Learning the names of coworkers as quickly as possible

▶ Asking questions to clarify information and asking for help as needed

▶ Taking notes to show interest and to assure that you recall critical information

▶ Taking initiative and being proactive

▶ Arriving on time, if not early; leaving on time or later than required; demonstrating time flexibility when possible

▶ Demonstrating responsibility by being at scheduled activities and following through on assignments

▶ Avoiding involvement in office politics and gossip

▶ Conducting a minimal amount of personal business on company time

◗ Getting involved with after work functions

◗ Demonstrating good manners by saying "thank you," "please," and so forth as appropriate

◗ Remaining organized by utilizing instruments such as daily and weekly planners

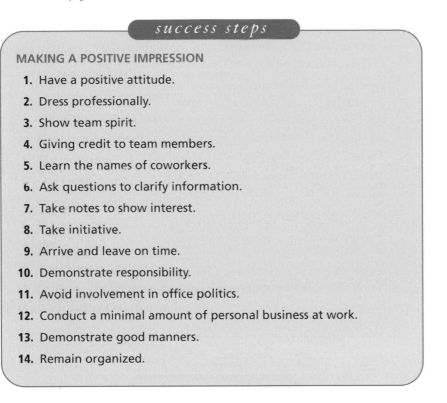

success steps

MAKING A POSITIVE IMPRESSION

1. Have a positive attitude.

2. Dress professionally.

3. Show team spirit.

4. Giving credit to team members.

5. Learn the names of coworkers.

6. Ask questions to clarify information.

7. Take notes to show interest.

8. Take initiative.

9. Arrive and leave on time.

10. Demonstrate responsibility.

11. Avoid involvement in office politics.

12. Conduct a minimal amount of personal business at work.

13. Demonstrate good manners.

14. Remain organized.

7

ATTITUDE COUNTS

Having a positive attitude can make a difference in your pursuit of professional success by contributing to the overall atmosphere on the job. A positive work environment:

◗ makes the work environment more pleasant

◗ allows for more creativity

◗ promotes a teamwork environment

◗ creates a more productive environment

It can be difficult to maintain a positive outlook, however, in the workplace, where not everything goes right all the time. Negativity in the workplace is a reality. Although employers can influence employee attitudes, it is the responsibility of every employee to respond positively to less-than-ideal situations. The following are some suggestions on how this can be accomplished:

▶ **Learn from challenges.** When a problem occurs, consider it as a challenge that can be effectively dealt with. Use the challenge as a learning opportunity to develop methods for addressing this type of issue.

▶ **Offer solutions.** If you believe that improvements can be made, offer them in the interest of improving the situation and with a constructive and positive attitude.

▶ **Remind yourself of positive accomplishments.** If you are feeling overwhelmed, take a piece of paper and draw a line down the middle. On one side, write what needs to be accomplished. On the other side, begin a list of what has been accomplished. Seeing the "accomplished" list grow can help you feel a positive sense of satisfaction.

▶ **Monitor your "inner voice."** Realize the importance of what you tell yourself. Brandi (n.d., p. 2) tells us to "recognize the power of positive self-talk. Often our internal chatter is negative." Reprogram your own chatter to be more positive.

▶ **Do not wallow in negativity.** Focus on being creative to solve the issues rather than spending time in exuding negative energy or wallowing in that of others.

▶ **Keep situations in perspective.** Avoid overdramatizing situations and excessive worrying. These feelings are rarely (if ever) helpful. Many times, situations are not as bad as they seem, and solutions are attainable. Recognize needs for improvement, but view these situations as opportunities for growth—this is one way to remain positive.

▶ **Avoid joining in on the office gossip.** Gossip is destructive and can negatively impact attitudes and create an untrusting environment. Gossip "creates animosity, tension, and ill will" (Norris, 2000–2001, p. 2). Instead of gossiping, rechannel your energy into something positive. Remember, also, that gossip can backfire—it may haunt you in negative ways in the future.

success steps

MAINTAINING A POSITIVE ATTITUDE

1. Learn from challenges.
2. Offer solutions.
3. Remind yourself of positive accomplishments.

4. Monitor your "inner voice."

5. Do not wallow in negativity.

6. Keep situations in perspective.

7. Avoid joining in on the office gossip.

DEALING WITH DIFFICULT PEOPLE IN THE WORKPLACE

As in your personal life, you will also encounter difficult people at work. The difference with difficult coworkers, supervisors, or clients is that typically, you cannot simply ignore or dismiss them. Successful professionals have learned the skills required to work productively with various personalities and behaviors, including those that are sometimes difficult.

DEALING WITH DIFFICULT PEERS

Some individuals are simply irritating. Given this, there will be any number of times throughout your life when you will encounter such folks, including in your work environment. Dealing effectively with difficult people requires accepting the reality of their personalities and/or behaviors. But it is important to realize that not all annoying behavior needs attention or should be responded to. As long as someone's behavior does not disrupt the quality and quantity of work, the issue probably can be left alone. Examples of behaviors that may be annoying, but not necessarily disruptive, include poor hygiene, poor manners, and similar conduct that has little impact on productivity.

Some personality types and behaviors, however, do require attention and should not be accepted in the workplace. Examples of these include excessive socializing, emotional outbursts, engaging in inappropriate soliciting (such as for political or religious causes), plagiarism, and taking credit for another person's work.

Addressing these issues can be difficult, but ignoring them may be detrimental to overall job satisfaction and to company productivity. Consider the following suggestions for dealing with difficult people in the workplace (Heathfield, n.d.):

▶ **Assess your own behavior.** Make sure that you are not the problem—examine yourself. Your personality and/or behaviors may be contributing to the situation.

Be aware of behavior in the workplace that might be annoying or distracting to others.

7

▶ **Get an outside perspective.** Talk to a friend or trusted coworker to get his or her perspective of the situation. Another individual's opinion may not only provide useful information but also help determine a solution. Be careful, however, that seeking an outside perspective is not misconstrued as gossip.

▶ **Address the issue with the individual.** Have a private conversation with the person you are having difficulties with. Use "I" messages: "An 'I' message uses the template 'I *feel* [name the feeling] *when you* [describe the behavior] *because* [state the consequences or reasons for your feelings]' and is clear and direct. The sequence is critical: state your feeling first, then their part described in behavior terms, then what it means to you. If you begin with 'You . . .,' everything after that will be deflected and they'll probably say 'You . . .' also" (Robin, 1997–2004, p. 2).

▶ **Follow up as appropriate.** Conduct a follow-up if necessary. If the person's behavior has improved, no follow-up may be required. If change has not occurred, ask yourself how badly you want the change to take place. Will follow-up help the situation or escalate it unnecessarily?

▶ **Seek assistance if necessary.** Involve others if it is necessary to readdress the issue. You may want to include your supervisor or the individual's supervisor. Involving coworkers who have been affected by the behavior(s) at issue may also be helpful. A group approach may be more successful in convincing the individual that his or her behavior is not appropriate and that it is affecting many people. Whenever it is necessary to address problem behavior, first speak to the individual directly and be sure to follow the company's chain of command in the event you need to address the situation further.

▶ **Take additional action if necessary.** If all efforts have failed, the following are your remaining options:

  ▶ Limit the person's access to you. This is only possible if your work productivity is not affected by limited contact with the individual.

  ▶ Request a transfer to another division or department within the organization.

  ▶ Seek employment elsewhere.

Most importantly, you must consider the effects the situation may have on your stress level and your work. Based on this assessment, you can make wise choices.

success steps

DEALING WITH DIFFICULT PEERS

1. Assess your own behavior.
2. Get an outside perspective.
3. Address the issue with the individual.
4. Follow up as appropriate.
5. Seek assistance if necessary.
6. Take additional action if necessary.

REFLECTION QUESTIONS

- What person in your personal or professional life do you have difficulty with?
- Is there anything you can do to deal more effectively with the situation?

DEALING WITH A DIFFICULT SUPERVISOR

Your options for dealing with a difficult supervisor are different from those of dealing with a difficult peer. Handling a difficult supervisor is one of the most challenging, if not the most challenging, situations an employee can face. Difficult supervisors may demonstrate such behaviors as micromanaging, being overly controlling, rudeness, exhibiting sexist or racist attitudes, or being incompetent (Hansen, n.d.[c]). Although you may work under good supervisors during most of your career, you probably will encounter a bad one eventually. "One study found that almost 80 percent of the employees surveyed identified their supervisor as a lousy manager. And almost 70 percent in that 2001 study conducted by Delta Road stated that their immediate superior had 'no clue' what to do to become a good manager. Author Harvey Hornstein, Ph.D., estimates that 90 percent of the U.S. workforce has been subjected to abusive behavior at some time" (Hansen, n.d.[c], p. 1).

Consider the following guidelines for coping with a difficult or ineffective supervisor (Hansen, n.d.[c]):

- **Maintain your professionalism.** Act professionally in all situations. Demonstrate respect for your supervisor and behave as you would in any other professional encounter.

- **Speak assertively.** Do not confront your supervisor in an emotionally charged attack. Remain calm, state your position in a conversational tone, and use "I" statements to identify your feelings (as suggested for addressing a difficult peer) to avoid sounding accusatory.

- **Use a problem-solving approach.** Consider scheduling a meeting with your supervisor to discuss the elements of his or her behavior that you find difficult. Approach the issue with the attitude that you

7

are willing to do what is necessary to improve the situation. Avoid exhibiting an angry, blaming, or defensive attitude.

▌ **Go to your supervisor first.** Make every attempt to resolve the issue with your supervisor before going up the chain of command. Do not go to your supervisor's supervisor, unless as a last resort.

▌ **Vent frustrations outside of work.** It is normal to have frustrations and it is healthy to vent them. However, do so with a neutral and supportive third party. Do not express your frustrations and anger to coworkers.

▌ **Be patient.** Even if your supervisor has agreed that change is necessary and has promised to make changes, do not expect your supervisor to change immediately.

▌ **Be aware of other opportunities.** If your supervisor cannot or will not change, watch for opportunities to transfer to another department within the company. In some cases, you may also want to watch for opportunities outside the company.

▌ **Do not just ignore the situation.** It is important to address the situation in some manner. Simply ignoring problems with your supervisor can affect your performance at work as well as negatively affect both your physical and mental health.

▌ **Do a self-assessment.** Be aware of your own behaviors that you can change to improve your performance and relationships on the job. However, be objective in your evaluation and do not blame yourself for problems caused by an ineffective supervisor.

▌ **Document your observations.** Consider keeping a journal that documents your supervisor's inappropriate behavior.

▌ **Document your accomplishments.** Keep a record of your accomplishments as well as copies of work that you produce.

success steps

DEALING WITH DIFFICULT SUPERVISORS

1. Maintain your professionalism.

2. Speak assertively.

3. Use a problem-solving approach.

4. Go to your supervisor first.

5. Vent frustrations outside of work.

6. Be patient.

7. Be aware of other opportunities.

8. Do not just ignore the situation.

9. Do a self-assessment.

10. Document your observations.

11. Document your accomplishments.

Documenting your observations and your accomplishments will be useful in the event that such information is later required by upper management or—in extreme cases—for legal reasons.

RESOLVING CONFLICT

Interactions between disparate personalities and behaviors can lead to a variety of conflicts in the workplace. Conflict in the workplace can occur for a number of reasons, including employees feeling that they are being taken advantage of, unrealistic expectations, misunderstandings, and conflicting goals and values (Fiore, 1999–2004). Resolving conflicts effectively is important to maintaining a positive working environment.

Addressing potential conflict in its early stages and defusing it by using effective communication techniques contributes to a pleasant work environment.

Strong communication skills are critical in successful conflict resolution. By making "I" statements and actively listening, many potential conflicts can be avoided and actual conflicts can be minimized. The following are further suggestions on resolving workplace conflicts (Portland Community College, n.d.):

▶ **Clearly identify the problem.** Ensure that the problem has been identified correctly. Doing so ensures that efforts to resolve the issue will be appropriately directed, thus contributing to a more expeditious and effective solution. You do not want to address a problem only to find out that it is not actually the issue.

▶ **Determine whether it is worth addressing.** Determine how serious the problem is and how frequently it occurs. Making an accurate and fair assessment helps determine whether the problem is worth addressing.

▶ **Evaluate resolution methods.** Consider the simplest way to resolve the problem. Methods include sharing concerns during a conversation, apologizing, holding a meeting, or seeking mediation. Mediation, which involves a neutral third party who moderates discussion between the conflicted parties, is often an effective method for resolving disputes.

7

Exercising is a positive way to alleviate stress.

DEALING WITH STRESS EFFECTIVELY

Situations such as dealing with a difficult supervisor or coworker and resolving conflict can add to the more typical type of stress that is experienced on the job. Stress at work is a topic not to be underestimated (Reed Consulting, 2005). Research indicates that one in five employees suffers from stress at some stage in his or her working life and that stress contributes significantly to absence from work. In addition, stress on the job contributes to health issues such as heart disease and stroke.

Stress at work occurs for various reasons, including dealing with time pressures, work relationships, long work hours, and office politics (Reed Consulting, 2005). Recognizing work stressors and minimizing them when possible is important for your overall mental and physical health, which can significantly impact your ability to perform your job.

The following are general steps for being proactive in dealing with stress (McGarvey, 2001):

▶ **Say "no" when appropriate.** Be aware of your own time constraints and say "no" to deadlines and projects when necessary. It is important to have realistic expectations about work demands and about your abilities to meet them. Saying "no" is preferable to continuing to take on more work and risking possible failure and added stress.

▶ **Be organized.** Being organized allows your time to be used more effectively, providing for more to be accomplished in a shorter period. Disorganization can create added pressures and stress.

▶ **Use time wisely during the day.** Eliminate the need to rush. Arrive early when possible and set your schedule to eliminate rushing. Refer to Chapter 5 to review methods for effective time management.

▶ **Develop sources of positive energy.** Reduce areas in your life and at work that drain your energy. Create positive energy in your life by making time for relaxation and hobbies and activities that generate positive energy.

▶ **Be healthy.** Exercise and establish healthy eating habits. Wholesome food gives you more energy, and exercise helps counteract stress. Get adequate rest each night.

▶ **Take care of yourself.** Find time in your day to relax. Pamper yourself each day in small ways. Get a massage or take a hot bath.

▶ **Look for learning opportunities.** Try to view issues at work as opportunities rather than as sources of stress. Your mind is a powerful tool. Thinking positively about an experience may make it less stressful. Do not see or expect problems or stresses where they may not exist.

▶ **Do not do it alone.** Ask for help and delegate tasks when possible. Surround yourself with individuals who are positive, have high energy, and are willing to take on challenges.

▶ **Create a peaceful office environment.** Surround yourself with items that center you and remind you of what is important.

▶ **Get physical.** At times of stress, do something physical. Take deep breaths, go for a quick walk, count to 10. Create calm within yourself.

▶ **Use energy wisely.** Focus on what is positive and good. Put the stress into perspective. Consider whether the issue is worth the negative energy that you are putting into it.

▶ **Find the humor.** Having a sense of humor in the workplace is critical to relieving everyday stress.

success steps

DEALING WITH STRESS

1. Say "no" when appropriate.
2. Be organized.
3. Use time in the day wisely.
4. Develop sources of positive energy.
5. Be healthy.
6. Take care of yourself.
7. Look for learning opportunities.
8. Do not do it alone.
9. Get physical.
10. Use energy wisely.
11. Find the humor.

▶ REFLECTION QUESTIONS

- How effective are you at dealing with your daily personal and professional stressors?
- What can you do in your life to eliminate or diminish these stressors?

? CRITICAL THINKING QUESTION

7–2. How critical are exercise and rest to one's overall pursuit of success?

PERFORMANCE APPRAISALS, RAISES, AND PROMOTIONS

Performance appraisal systems vary, depending upon the company, but their general purpose is to provide employees with written feedback regarding their work. In well-managed organizations, employees are never surprised by what is presented to them in the performance appraisal because they have received verbal feedback on an ongoing basis. In most organizations, appraisal results are used to determine pay increases and other rewards (Archer North & Associates, 2004).

Companies usually try to make their appraisal system successful, but not all systems work well. When complaints are lodged regarding performance appraisals, they often concern the type of assessment scale used and/or inconsistencies in what the employee has been told versus what is presented in writing. If inconsistency is an issue, employees should voice their concerns and address them in a professional manner. In some cases, it may be necessary to an employee to accept the appraisal results and improve areas in which his performance is weak. If this is the case, establishing weekly meetings with your supervisor to review your progress in these areas can improve future appraisals.

Often, raises are directly linked to performance appraisals. Consider the following suggestions when requesting a raise (Hansen, n.d.[d]):

▶ **Document your accomplishments.** Prove your value by providing examples of your work and showing what you have contributed to the company. Provide objective evidence supporting your request for a raise.

▶ **Ask for raises in a professional manner.** When asking for a raise, always maintain a professional attitude and demeanor. Remain objective and assertive.

▶ **Make sure your request is realistic.** Research what others in your field are being paid and make sure that your expectations fall within appropriate parameters.

▶ **Consider other compensation.** Be prepared to consider other options, such as benefits in exchange for monetary increases. Depending on the company's budget, benefits may be proposed as an option.

▶ **Use negotiation skills.** Practice your negotiation skills with a friend or family member. Know what you will and will not accept, as well as your reasons. Consider including a "bargaining chip" (something you are willing to give up) in your request.

▶ **Ask for raises in the right environment.** Request a raise in a scheduled meeting. Do not ask in the hallway or at another unscheduled event.

▶ **Make your wishes known.** If you believe you deserve a raise, ask for it. Don't hound your employer if it does not happen right away, but do stay consistent without being annoying.

▶ **Be proactive for the future.** If you do not get a raise, ask your employer what you can do to earn one.

success steps

REQUESTING A RAISE

1. Document your accomplishments.
2. Ask for raises in a professional manner.
3. Make sure your request is realistic.
4. Consider other compensation in lieu of a raise.
5. Use negotiation skills.
6. Ask in the right environment.
7. Make your wishes known.
8. Be proactive for the future.

Many employees begin in entry-level positions with the expectation and aspiration of moving up the ladder in the organization. A history of positive performance appraisals helps establish you as a strong choice for promotion. Other strategies to facilitate a promotion include the following (Hansen, n.d.[c]):

▶ **Establish relationships.** Establish relationships with individuals in the organization who can mentor you and promote you within the company.

▶ **Document your accomplishments and contributions.** Keep a record of your accomplishments that contribute to the company's bottom line.

▶ **Network within the organization.** Reach out to as many individuals in the company as possible. Demonstrate to them your accomplishments, strengths, and skills.

▶ **Demonstrate creativity.** Demonstrate your ability to be creative and innovative in your current position.

▶ **Demonstrate loyalty.** Show your loyalty and commitment to the organization through your actions and work.

▶ **Form positive relationships.** Establish a good working relationship with your current supervisor. Your supervisor should be your strongest supporter for further advancement.

▶ **Seek learning opportunities.** Find opportunities to expand your knowledge and skills. The more you can offer a company, the more valuable you become to it.

▶ **Take initiative.** Volunteer to take on more responsibility when possible.

7

▶ **Be responsible.** Earn a reputation for being a reliable employee.

▶ **Be professional.** Present yourself as a professional at all times. Actions and attire speak volumes.

▶ **Work collaboratively.** Build a reputation of being a team player.

success steps

MOVING AHEAD IN AN ORGANIZATION

1. Establish relationships within the company.
2. Document your accomplishments and contributions.
3. Network within the organization.
4. Demonstrate creativity.
5. Demonstrate loyalty.
6. Form positive relationships.
7. Seek learning opportunities.
8. Take initiative.
9. Be responsible.
10. Be professional.
11. Work collaboratively.

▶ REFLECTION QUESTIONS

- What are your professional goals and aspirations?
- What steps will you take to reach these goals?

? CRITICAL THINKING QUESTION

7–3. What would you say to the following statement: "Performance appraisals should be taken with a grain of salt"?

WORKPLACE ETIQUETTE DO'S AND DON'TS

Your professional image is significant to achieving success and to earning raises and promotions. Your image is as important as your skills and knowledge, because it reflects on the company, and your behavior is a crucial part of that image. Simply put, employees who dress and act professionally are more likely to receive salary increases and promotions. The professional image that you exhibited during the interviewing process should be demonstrated on a daily basis.

"Successful impressions also require successful behavior" (Ritter, 2002, p. 2). The following behavior is important to creating the impression that you deserve raises and promotions (Bayer & Mallett, 2005):

▶ **Be approachable.** Say "hello" to coworkers you pass in the hallway and acknowledge their presence whenever possible and appropriate.

▶ **Avoid gossip.** Do not get involved in office gossip. Doing so is unproductive and promotes a distrusting relationship with others.

▶ **Follow the company's rules.** Those who break the rules are not only being rude but are demonstrating unprofessional behavior.

▶ **Use recommended telephone etiquette.** Follow guidelines regarding proper telephone etiquette that demonstrate professionalism.

▶ **Be aware of time.** Be prompt, but not so early that you appear to be wasting time or have nothing else to do. Do not keep others waiting, as it can send the message that you do not understand the value of their time.

▶ **Demonstrate manners during interactions.** Avoid interrupting others unless the interruption is valid and important to the discussion. Choose your words carefully and be tactful.

▶ **Make appointments.** Never walk into an office and sit down without asking permission or being invited to do so.

▶ **Return borrowed items.** Keep a record of items you have borrowed and return them to the correct owner in a timely manner. Consider a small token of appreciation, such as a thank-you note or tag attached to the item.

▶ **Keep a professional environment.** Treat your office space as an area that promotes professionalism. Avoid displaying personal items that make political or religious statements.

success steps

BEHAVIORS FOR SUCCESS

1. Be approachable.
2. Avoid gossip.
3. Follow the company's rules.
4. Use recommended telephone etiquette.
5. Be aware of time.
6. Demonstrate manners during interactions.
7. Make appointments.
8. Return borrowed items.
9. Keep a professional environment.

7

BUSINESS LUNCH MEETINGS

Business lunches offer another opportunity to demonstrate your professionalism. Depending on your position, business lunches may be commonplace or rare. Regardless of how frequently you attend such events, you must be prepared to present a positive image during them. Consider the following tips for business lunch etiquette (Franz, n.d., & Turner, 2004):

▶ **Turn off your cell phone.** Ensure that your cell phone is off or in vibrate mode prior to entering the meeting place. If you must receive a call turning the lunch meeting, inform the attendees that this is the case and apologize in advance. If the call occurs, excuse yourself from the table to answer it. Only urgent business calls or emergency calls should be received. Make the call as short as possible.

▶ **Always be on time.** Arrive punctually, and when you arrive, offer firm handshakes and professional greetings to individuals at the table. If introductions have not occurred, introduce yourself and other attendees as needed.

▶ **Use appropriate table manners.** Sit down and immediately place your napkin in your lap. If you excuse yourself during the meeting, place your napkin on the left side of your plate, as this indicates to the server that you are not finished. When you are done, signal that you are finished by placing your napkin on the right side of the plate and your fork and knife across the plate at "4 o'clock." Avoid placing your elbows on the table. Never talk with your mouth full. Give less attention to your food and more attention to the individuals at the meeting.

▶ **Order modestly and wisely.** If you are not paying for the bill, do not order the most expensive item on the menu. Avoid ordering items that are messy to eat, such as ribs, wings, or spaghetti.

▶ **Avoid alcoholic beverages.** It is a good rule of thumb to avoid alcoholic beverages during a business lunch. Never order alcohol if your host has not done so. If you do have a glass of wine, have only one.

▶ **Be courteous to the wait staff.** Act professionally toward the wait staff. Remember that the image you convey represents that of your organization.

▶ **Appear confident.** Help yourself feel confident by dressing professionally. If you are nervous during the meeting, do not overcompensate by talking too much or too little. Listen to others at the table and join the conversation when appropriate. Small talk is appropriate at a business lunch, and you must be prepared to participate. If this is a skill that is difficult for you, practice! Never gossip during a business lunch.

▶ **Follow others' cues.** Do not rush the meeting if you are not in charge. It is not up to you to conclude when the meeting should end.

▶ **Work out the finances ahead of time.** If you called the meeting, you are responsible for the bill. If the meeting is a joint meeting, then determine ahead of time whether the bill will be split. Never work out the financial issues at the table. If you do not pay for the lunch, thank the person who does.

▶ **Know the appropriate use of table settings.** Bread and salad plates are to the left of your place setting, and your drinking glass is to the right. Use utensils from the outside in. The dessert fork is by the dessert plate or at the top of the place setting.

Proper etiquette is critical during business lunch meetings. For example, taking a cell phone call is not appropriate unless it is related to the meeting or a significant emergency.

---

success steps

ETIQUETTE FOR BUSINESS MEALS

1. Turn off your cell phone.
2. Always be on time.
3. Use appropriate table manners.
4. Order modestly and wisely.
5. Avoid alcoholic beverages.
6. Be courteous to the wait staff.
7. Appear confident.
8. Follow others' cues.
9. Work out the finances ahead of time.
10. Know the appropriate use of table settings.

---

apply it

Role-Playing a Lunch Meeting

GOAL: To simulate and experience a lunch meeting.

STEP 1: Set up a lunch meeting scenario in the classroom. Provide a table set with the appropriate utensils, napkins, plates, and so on. Have menus available for making selections. Serve food if possible. Select eight students in the class to play the role of the lunch attendees. Select one student to be the server. The other students will be silent observers. Select one student to play the supervisor who has called the luncheon, and give this student the purpose for the meeting and the topics to be discussed. In addition to business conversation, play out issues regarding cell phones, leaving the table, introductions, napkin placement, fork use, and so forth.

continued

7

continued

STEP 2: Role-play the lunch meeting from start to finish. Have the lunch go for about 15 to 30 minutes, with each participant playing the role provided to him or her.

STEP 3: At the end of the lunch meeting, have all students evaluate the situation and discuss what was learned.

COMPANY PARTIES

Most company parties offer an excellent opportunity to get to know and network with colleagues. During these events, individuals can promote themselves and their abilities as well as enjoy their coworkers' company. Following are some basic rules for making the best of a company party (Hansen, n.d.[f]):

▶ **Exhibit professional behavior.** Although the party is a social event, never forget who the attendees are or that your behavior will make either a negative or a positive impression on your colleagues.

▶ **Attend company events whenever possible.** Your presence makes a statement regarding your desire to be involved with the company, and if you don't attend, you are losing networking opportunities.

▶ **Enjoy yourself, but remain professional.** Drinking too much and/or making a fool of yourself will not present the image you want your employers to see.

▶ **Dress appropriately.** Find out what attire is appropriate for the event, and then choose an outfit that is fitting to the occasion, yet is fairly conservative. Avoid overly revealing or otherwise inappropriate attire.

▶ **Learn how to engage in small talk.** This is an essential skill at a company function. Avoid talking only about business. As always, avoid gossip. Avoid topics that stir peoples' emotions, such as politics and religion.

▶ **Be a good listener.** Allow others to talk about themselves. Learn as much as you can about your employers and other coworkers. Demonstrate interest by asking questions.

▶ **Greet people appropriately.** Keep your right hand free throughout the event so that you can shake hands during introductions. Introduce yourself to people you do not know.

▶ **Drink and eat in moderation.** Avoid becoming intoxicated if alcoholic beverages are served. Eat politely and in conservative amounts.

▶ **Make a professional exit.** Do not be the last person to leave the party. When you do leave, always thank your host.

success steps

ETIQUETTE FOR COMPANY PARTIES

1. Exhibit professional behavior.
2. Attend company events whenever possible.
3. Enjoy yourself, but remain professional.
4. Dress appropriately.
5. Learn how to engage in small talk.
6. Be a good listener.
7. Greet people appropriately.
8. Drink and eat in moderation.
9. Make a professional exit.

REFLECTION QUESTIONS

- What issue(s) about lunch meetings and company parties concern you?
- How can you be proactive in dealing with these concerns?

CRITICAL THINKING QUESTION

7–4. Is it ever appropriate to let your guard down at a company lunch meeting or party? Explain your answer.

apply it

Research and Presentation

GOAL: *To increase your understanding of the various topics discussed in this chapter.*

STEP 1: Select one or two topics from the chapter that you want to research. Other class members should select other topics.

STEP 2: Research your topic(s) using the articles referenced in this chapter and other resources available on the Internet and/or at the library.

STEP 3: Write a brief report on what you learned from this activity and be prepared to make a presentation to the class.

STEP 4: Consider placing this report in your Learning Portfolio.

CHAPTER SUMMARY

This chapter addressed aspects of professionalism in the workplace, many of which go beyond the office setting. Professional behaviors that promote a positive impression in the workplace were summarized, and you learned effective methods for requesting raises and moving ahead in an organization. You also learned strategies for addressing coworkers' and supervisors' inappropriate behavior and steps for resolving conflict. In addition, this chapter addressed etiquette for work-related activities in which you may become involved, such as business meals and company parties. Overall, professionalism, a positive attitude, and being proactive were emphasized as key elements for success.

POINTS TO KEEP IN MIND

In this chapter, several main points were discussed in detail:

- Technological advancements offer options to employers and employees regarding where and how work will be performed. These options include flex time, compressed work schedules, job sharing, and telecommuting.
- Making a good first impression is important for overall job success and for establishing positive relationships with supervisor and coworkers.
- Although employers can influence employee attitudes, it is the responsibility of every employee to try and overcome negativity and remain positive.
- Successful professionals have learned the skills required to work productively with various personalities and behaviors.
- Dealing with difficult people is a challenge, but utilizing some basic communication tools can make your approach more effective.
- Resolving conflict effectively is important to achieving a positive work environment.
- Recognizing work stresses and minimizing them when possible is important for your overall mental and physical health, both of which significantly impact your ability to perform your job.
- A history of positive performance appraisals can help establish you as a strong candidate for promotion.
- Demonstrating professionalism through your attire and behavior—that is, maintaining a professional image—significantly impacts management decisions regarding raises and promotions.

LEARNING OBJECTIVES REVISITED

Review the learning objectives for this chapter and rate your level of achievement for each objective using the rating scale provided. For each objective on which you do not rate yourself as a 3, outline a plan of action that you will take to fully achieve the objective. Include a time frame for this plan.

1 = did not successfully achieve objective

2 = understand what is needed, but need more study or practice

3 = achieved learning objective thoroughly

	1	2	3
List areas that should be evaluated when assessing a job offer.	☐	☐	☐
List qualities that employers seek when hiring new employees.	☐	☐	☐
List problem personality types and behaviors that can be encountered in the workplace.	☐	☐	☐
List and explain the steps involved when dealing with difficult people.	☐	☐	☐
Discuss the pros and cons of telecommuting.	☐	☐	☐
Explain how good first impressions can be achieved at a new job.	☐	☐	☐
Understand methods for overcoming negativity and remaining positive.	☐	☐	☐
Explain methods for coping with a bad or ineffective supervisor.	☐	☐	☐
Discuss how to resolve workplace conflict.	☐	☐	☐
Understand the effects of stress and discuss how stress can be dealt with proactively.	☐	☐	☐
Describe the purpose of performance appraisals.	☐	☐	☐
Explain the do's and don'ts to requesting a raise and obtaining a promotion.	☐	☐	☐
Discuss positive and negative office behaviors.	☐	☐	☐
Discuss the issues that should be considered when attending a business lunch meeting and a company party.	☐	☐	☐

Steps to Achieve Unmet Objectives

Steps	Due Date
1. _____	_____
2. _____	_____
3. _____	_____
4. _____	

SUGGESTED ITEMS FOR LEARNING PORTFOLIO

Refer to the "Developing Portfolios" section at the front of this textbook for more information on learning portfolios.

▶ Telecommuting Opportunities: This activity will help you explore telecommuting opportunities in your field.

▶ Research and Presentation: The goal of this activity is to provide an opportunity to investigate a topic of your choice related to professionalism in the workplace.

▶ Role-Playing a Lunch Meeting: This activity will provide an opportunity to practice lunch meeting etiquette.

● REFERENCES

Archer North & Associates. (2004). Introduction performance appraisal [electronic version]. Archer North Performance Appraisal System. Retrieved April 14, 2005, from http://www.performance-appraisal .com/intro.htm

Bayer, L., & Mallett, K. (2005). The etiquette ladies: Top ten "unquestionably rude" office behaviors [electronic version]. Retrieved April 13, 2005, from http://www.canoe.ca/LifewiseWorkEtiquette/ eti_work.html

Brandi, J. (n.d.). Creating a positive employee attitude in the workplace [electronic version]. Retrieved April 13, 2005, from http://www .sideroad.com/Management/employee_attitude.html

Fiore, T. (1999–2004). Resolving workplace conflict: 4 ways to a win-win solution [electronic version]. Retrieved April 19, 2005, from http:// www.businessknowhow.com/manage/resolve.htm

Franz, C. (n.d.). Business lunch etiquette [electronic version]. Retrieved April 14, 2005, from http://www.sideroad.com/Business_etiquette/ busines-lunch-etiquette.html

Greenspan, R. (2002). Telecommuting gains ground [electronic version]. Retrieved April 14, 2005, from http://www.clickz.com/stats/sectors/ professional/article.php/1429771

Hansen, K. (n.d.[a]). Making your case for telecommuting: How to convince the boss [electronic version]. Retrieved April 14, 2005, from http://www.quintcareers.com/telecommuting_options.html

Hansen, R. S. (n.d.[b]). Is job flexibility right for you? A quintessential careers quiz [electronic version]. Retrieved April 14, 2005, from http://www.quintcareers.com/job_flexibility_quiz.html

Hansen, R. S. (n.d.[c]). Your first days working at a new job: 20 tips to help you make a great impression [electronic version]. Retrieved April 14, 2005, from http://www.quintcareers.com/first_days_working.html

Hansen, R. S. (n.d.[c]). Do's and don'ts of dealing with a bad boss [electronic version]. Retrieved April 14, 2005, from http://www .quintcareers.com/bad_boss-dos-donts.html

Hansen, R. S. (n.d.[d]). Do's and don'ts of requesting a raise [electronic version]. Retrieved April 14, 2005, from http://www.quintcareers .com/requesting_raise-dos-donts.html

Hansen, R. S. (n.d.[e]). Moving up the ladder: 10 strategies for getting yourself promoted [electronic version]. Retrieved April 14, 2005, from http://www.quintcareers.com/getting_promoted_strategies.html

Hansen, R. S., & Hansen, K. (n.d.[f]). Your first days working at a new job: 20 tips to help you make a great impression. Retrieved June 22, 2006, from http://www.quintcareers.com/first_days_working.html

Heathfield, S. M. (n.d.). Rise above the fray: Options for dealing with difficult people at work. Five tips for dealing with difficult people [electronic version]. Retrieved April 19, 2005, from http:// humanresources .about.com/od/workrelationships/a/ difficultpeople_2.htm

Marquette University Career Services Center. (2003–2004). Top qualities & skills employers seek [electronic version]. Retrieved April 14, 2005, from http://www.marquettte.edu/csc/students/documents/ Topskillsemployersseek.pdf

McGarvey, J. (2000). The top 10 ways to eliminate stress [electronic version]. CoachVille Resource Center. Retrieved April 20, 2005, from http://topten.org/public/FB/BF123.html

Norris, B. (2000–2001). Overcoming negativity in the workplace [electronic version]. Retrieved April 13, 2005, from http://www .briannorris.com/artilces/overcomenegativity.html

Portland Community College. (n.d.). Resolving workplace problems [electronic version]. Retrieved April 19, 2005, from http://spot.pcc.edu/ ~rjacobs/career/resolving_workplace_problems.htm

Reed Consulting. (2005). Stress at work [electronic version]. Retrieved April 13, 2005, from http://reed.businesshr.net/docs/guides/ stress.html

Ritter, J. (2002). Impress for success: A professional approach to your professional image [electronic version]. *The Galt Global Review*. Retrieved April 13, 2005, from http://www.galtglobalreview.com/careers/ dress_to_impress.html

Robin, D. (1997–2004). The gentle art of confrontation [electronic version]. Retrieved April 19, 2005, from http://www.abetterworkplace .com/084.html

Turner, T. (2004). Business lunch etiquette 101 [electronic version]. Retrieved April 14, 2005, from http://www.marketingpower.com/ content20039C5627.php

7

CHAPTER OUTLINE

8

Career Advancement Strategies

LEARNING OBJECTIVES

By the end of this chapter, you will achieve the following objectives:

▶ Explain the importance of continued professional learning and development and its relationship to career advancement.

▶ Identify and locate resources for continued learning.

▶ Apply information about individual learning style to the professional development and career advancement strategies.

▶ Describe the professional supervision process and explain how supervision processes can be used to pursue professional development goals.

▶ Describe the skills, functions, and roles of management.

▶ Describe the skills of leadership.

▶ Compare and contrast management and leadership.

TOPIC SCENARIO

After graduating from school, Janna obtained an entry-level job with a local company and has been working in that position for several years. Janna likes her job and wants to remain with the company, but she feels it is time to advance to a management position. She has discussed her goals with her supervisor, who told Janna that she should develop her management and leadership skills. Janna set goals with her supervisor to pursue these suggestions.

Based on this scenario, answer the following questions:

▶ Where should Janna look for learning opportunities?

▶ How can Janna document her learning?

▶ How can Janna use the professional supervision process to support her efforts?

▶ What skills will Janna need to enhance her management skills?

▶ How do leadership skills differ from management skills?

▶ What will Janna need to do to develop her leadership skills?

STAYING AT THE FOREFRONT OF YOUR PROFESSION

Major factors in career advancement are being aware of current issues in your field, being able to apply new ideas to your work, and adapting to change in your profession. These abilities are achieved and demonstrated in several ways, which are discussed here.

LIFELONG LEARNING STRATEGIES AND PROFESSIONAL DEVELOPMENT

You have probably heard the saying that learning does not end at graduation. Your ability to continue learning contributes to your effectiveness in daily activities as well as to your career advancement in the form of promotions and the assumption of leadership roles. Both of these aspects of career advancement will be discussed in this chapter.

LIFELONG CAREER LEARNING AND STAYING CURRENT

There are many sources to tap to help you remain current in your field. Recall the information from Chapter 4, which focused on information literacy. The methods discussed in that chapter will be useful for the topics explored here. Consider the following sources of information, all of which can be used to support your continuing professional development.

PROFESSIONAL ORGANIZATIONS

Professional organizations are often an excellent source of information that will keep you current in your field. Membership in a professional organization offers the following benefits, all of which provide opportunity for continued learning.

▶ **Broad-based information.** A professional organization's primary task is to serve the profession it represents and keep its membership informed. Consequently, up-to-date information from all areas of the profession is typically available from such groups. For example, The American Occupational Therapy Association has specialized groups focused on education, practice issues, and political events that affect the field. A broad base of information allows members to access information in a variety of areas.

▶ **In-depth information.** In addition to a wide range of information, professional organizations can also supply in-depth information on a particular topic. Individuals whose job it is to monitor specific areas of a field can offer detailed and comprehensive information on that area.

▶ **Publications.** Most professional organizations produce a professional journal or other publication containing current information and updates about their fields. Some organizations offer specialty publications in specific areas of interest.

▶ **Conferences and seminars.** Professional organizations usually offer some form of annual conference and may sponsor additional seminars throughout the year. Conferences typically offer a choice of workshops and presentations on a variety of topics.

▶ **Expert contacts.** Many professional organizations offer members access to experts in a variety of areas within the field. These individuals are available to share their expertise and may be consulted via telephone, e-mail, or standard mail.

▶ **Electronic resources.** Online articles, libraries, and communication tools are frequently maintained by professional organizations. Some may be available to members at no charge or for a reasonable fee.

8

▶ **Networking opportunities.** Attending conferences, participating in electronic discussion groups, and becoming involved in other ways with your professional organization can provide numerous networking opportunities. Take advantage of these to become acquainted with other members of your profession.

Professional organizations offer many opportunities for professional development, including seminars, focus groups, and networking with professional peers.

apply it

Your Professional Organization

GOAL: To learn more about your field's primary professional organization.

STEP 1: Research your field's primary professional organization. Obtain information regarding membership and its benefits. Often, professional organizations offer reduced membership fees to students.

STEP 2: Consider how you might use some of the member benefits in your professional development and to support your professional interests. Seriously consider becoming a member of the organization to take advantage of these support systems.

STEP 3: Create a section in your Learning Portfolio for professional development documentation and information.

ONLINE RESOURCES

In addition to the common search engines and other tools, the Internet provides opportunities for you to be automatically updated about a variety of subjects. The following tools are especially useful in maintaining contact with colleagues and staying informed regarding professional developments.

Listservs

A listserv is a tool that allows participants to post questions and comments to a group of individuals who, in turn, have the opportunity to respond with answers, comments, and solutions. Most listservs have guidelines for etiquette and rules for participation. Some may have a moderator whose job is to ensure that guidelines and rules are followed. You can often locate listservs in your field through your professional organization or based on suggestions from colleagues.

apply it

Professional Listservs

GOAL: To gain experience using a professional listserv.

STEP 1: Contact your professional organization and whether it monitors any member listservs. Or, conduct an Internet search using "_____ listserv" (insert your field in the blank) and explore your search results. If you select the latter option, you may want to check the listserv's reputation with your professional organization or another reliable source.

STEP 2: Select an appropriate listserv and sign up as a member. Participate in discussions and post questions.

STEP 3: Consider placing the information you receive from the listserv in your Learning Portfolio.

Databases and Online Libraries

Chapter 4 discussed obtaining resources via the deep Web, which can provide access to databases and other more obscure documents. Search databases and online specialty libraries for current articles and other literature related to you field.

Simulations

Several fields have online simulations available that provide virtual experiences of real-life professional situations. Follow the instructions in Chapter 4 for searching and locating simulations in your field.

8

APPLYING YOUR LEARNING PREFERENCES
TO CAREER DEVELOPMENT

Taking advantage of the way in which you learn most effectively can greatly enhance your career advancement, because if you seek educational opportunities that are suited to your learning style, you will enjoy the process more and thus retain the information better. For example, if you know that you are a hands-on learner, seeking simulations or seminars with an activity component will suit you better than simply listening to a lecture. If, however, you are an auditory learner, a lecture probably will meet your needs well.

success steps

USING OPPORTUNITIES FOR PROFESSIONAL DEVELOPMENT

1. Seek resources from professional organizations:
   - broad-based information
   - in-depth information
   - publications
   - conferences and seminars
   - expert contacts
   - electronic resources
   - networking opportunities
2. Use online resources:
   - listservs
   - databases and online libraries
   - simulations
3. Understand your learning style.
4. Learn from your supervisor, a mentor, or a coach.

apply it

Identifying Your Learning Style

GOAL: To gain insight into your learning style and how it can support your professional development.

STEP 1: Conduct an Internet search using "learning style inventory" as your search term. Locate an inventory you want to take and complete it. If you have previously completed a learning inventory, consider repeating the process, this time keeping career advancement and professional development in mind. Learning preferences can change over time and depending on what you are learning.

STEP 2: Review the results of the inventory. Add or modify information according to your experience and what you know about your learning patterns.

STEP 3: Make a list of professional education activities that are appropriate to your learning style. Consider using the Internet or professional organization resources to explore your choices.

STEP 4: Consider maintaining a list of professional learning activity ideas in your Learning Portfolio.

PROFESSIONAL CERTIFICATIONS AND LICENSURE

Professional development and continued learning is often linked with certifications and licenses that you must keep current in order to practice in your field. Examples of professionals who are required to maintain current certifications are teachers and nurses. Requirements to maintain current credentials typically include a specific number of continuing education hours that must be completed within a certain period. Each profession has its own requirements; review your field's guidelines. Regardless of the field, continuing education can support credentialing requirements and advance your career. Choose education opportunities that support your goals.

DOCUMENTING PROFESSIONAL DEVELOPMENT

It is critical to keep records of your professional development, including documentation of continuing education for licensure and certification purposes. Ensure that you receive course-completion documentation for each continuing education activity that you finish. This documentation should be on official stationery, such as letterhead, and include the number of hours completed and the signature of an authorized person.

THE PROFESSIONAL SUPERVISION PROCESS

Professional supervision involves numerous techniques, including teaching, directing, mentoring, and coaching. A common perception of supervision is that a supervisor "watches over" employees, but true professional supervision

8

is a complex process directed at developing employees' professional skills that facilitate their career advancement. As such, professional supervision is another tool for professional development.

DIRECTING

Directing is the process of leading someone through a task or activity, and there are times when direction is appropriate and necessary. Recent graduates, for example, who are new to the field often benefit from direct guidance. In addition, more experienced employees who are learning a new or advanced skill may also find direction through their learning process helpful. Although you should increase your ability to be independent whenever possible, asking for direction in certain situations demonstrates a realistic understanding of your skills and your job as well as your willingness to learn.

Direction may take the form of corrective feedback, or constructive criticism, which may be necessary when issues of safety, compliance with ethics and regulations, and similar concerns are at stake. Used appropriately, corrective feedback can be used to facilitate learning.

TEACHING

Teaching differs from directing in that teaching provides learners with information and skills that they will apply independently. Teaching can be, and usually is, a part of directing. As you assimilate the teaching of your supervisor, you will become more independent, decreasing your need for direction.

COACHING

Coaching is a technique in which someone (in this case, your supervisor) encourages, challenges, and supports the person being coached (you, in this scenario). The coaching approach is less like the teaching approach and more like the process that sports coaches use with their teams. The employee takes the lead in learning and applying the information while the supervisor guides by encouraging or challenging as appropriate.

MENTORING

Mentoring is a process that goes beyond technical aspects of the job and includes considerations of the employee's growth and development as a person as well as a professional. A mentor may engage in activities such as

©Digital Vision

Professional supervision offers a one-on-one opportunity for exploring areas for professional development. Working closely with your supervisor gives you the chance to set and pursue professional goals.

8

helping the mentee understand how to navigate corporate culture, determine which skills to develop to advance professionally, and expand the personal skills needed for success.

In the real world, supervisors are likely to use each of these methods on occasion, depending on the situation and the needs of the employee.

Your supervisor does not do all the work, however—you have responsibilities as a learner in this situation. Consider these actions you can take to make the most of your supervision experience (Berger, 2003):

▸ **Know yourself.** Acknowledge your strengths and weaknesses. Capitalize on your strengths and improve your weak areas through professional development.

▸ **Clearly state your needs and goals.** Let your supervisor know what motivates you, the type of direction you need, how you learn most effectively, and what your professional goals include.

▸ **Be open to learning.** Approach being supervised as an opportunity to learn and use your supervisor as a source of professional information. Actively involve yourself in the supervision process by asking questions and participating in discussion. Accept corrective feedback (constructive criticism) as helpful information intended to support your professional growth. Incorporate corrective feedback into your professional development goals.

▸ **Set goals.** Set goals based on what you wish to accomplish in your career. Identify areas of professional interest and seek the resources to pursue them. Discuss your career advancement plans with your supervisor so that he or she can assist you in this process.

▸ **Keep written records.** Keep written records of your supervision sessions, your goals, and your progress toward reaching them. Use your documentation to guide your supervision and career advancement.

8

success steps

GETTING THE MOST FROM SUPERVISION

1. Know yourself.
2. Clearly state your needs and goals.
3. Be open to learning.
4. Set goals.
5. Keep written records.

▸ REFLECTION QUESTION

- What are your professional goals?

❓ CRITICAL THINKING QUESTION

8–1. How could you best use supervision to reach your professional goals?

8

apply it

Supervision Goals

GOAL: **To set goals for enhancing your professional development and career advancement.**

Note: This activity is intended for use in the workplace. It may be adapted for academic advising or used in the student's current employment.

STEP 1: In an electronic or print document (select whichever is easier for you to use), create a table with five columns. From left to right, label the columns "Goal," "Steps/Time Frames," "Methods," "Revisions," and "Outcomes."

STEP 2: In the "Goals" column, write your long-term goal. In the "Steps/Time Frames" column, break your long-term goal into smaller steps. Assign a completion date to each step. In the "Methods" column, note resources and techniques you can use to achieve these steps and, ultimately, your goal.

STEP 3: Note any necessary revisions in the "Revisions" column. For example, if you need to adjust time frames or methods, record that information in this column. In the "Outcomes" column, keep a record of your results as you work toward your goal. You may find it more convenient to record certain pieces of information in a journal-style document.

STEP 4: Share your goal document(s) with your supervisor for input and support. Be sure to let your supervisor know how he or she can help you achieve your goal.

STEP 5: Consider placing your goals and related documentation in your Learning Portfolio.

PROMOTIONS AND CAREER ADVANCEMENT

Professional development activities are frequently directed at helping you move ahead in your field. Advancement into management and leadership positions requires the possession of specific skills in addition to technical expertise.

INTERPERSONAL SKILLS

The ability to relate effectively to colleagues at every level of an organization is critical to job success. Interpersonal skills become increasingly critical, however, with advancement to more senior levels of an organization, because management and leadership roles are typically more people oriented than strictly technical positions. Review Chapter 3 for an in-depth discussion of communication skills. Be aware that communication is a complex topic and that there are many additional resources you can tap to develop strong management and leadership skills. Elements such as emotional intelligence, team building, group dynamics, and others are subjects that are worth investigating.

©Digital Vision

Being able to work effectively with individuals at all levels of an organization requires interpersonal skills and is important to your career advancement.

8

apply it

Communication Techniques

GOAL: *To become familiar with advanced communication techniques.*

STEP 1: Create a list of communication skills and topics that you want to develop or about which you want to learn. Which might you wish to expand on to build your management and leadership skills? Consider exploring such topics as emotional

continued

continued

intelligence, group dynamics, assertiveness, effective questioning, and conflict resolution.

STEP 2: Conduct an Internet search using the skill(s) or topic(s) that you select. Create an electronic or print resource file of articles and other information from your search results.

STEP 3: Set goals and identify methods for applying the information you obtain and for practicing the skills that you learn. Keep a record of your progress.

STEP 4: Consider placing the resources, your goals, and progress notes in your Learning Portfolio.

MANAGEMENT

Management skills are a subset of interpersonal skills. They relate to the mission and purpose of an organization and help ensure that daily tasks are executed in a manner that contributes to organizational goals. Becoming a successful manager requires possessing these specific skills and being able to carry out certain functions. Managerial tasks include staffing, budgeting, ensuring adequate productivity, writing and implementing policy and procedure, and ensuring appropriate communication within a work unit and with other work units in the organization.

Management Skills

There are three major areas in which managers must be skilled to perform their duties effectively. Each of these areas can be elaborated upon, and much has been written on management skills. The following, however, is a summary of these skill sets (Allen, 1998a).

- **Technical skill.** Technical skill includes the ability to perform the job for which you were trained. For example, a computer programmer must be able to program a computer, and a medical assistant must know how to take an accurate medical history.

- **Human skill.** This is the ability to work effectively with people. Managers must be able to work successfully with the individuals they supervise as well as with an organization's upper management. Examples of human skills include communication and negotiation skills as well as the ability to work collaboratively.

- **Conceptual skill.** Conceptual skills are the ability to generate, apply, and carry out ideas. Examples include implementing new programs and interpreting policy and procedure.

Management Functions

The duties of a manager are directed at ensuring that the work unit functions efficiently and in keeping with organizational goals. Managers use their skills to carry out the following interrelated functions (Allen, 1998b).

- ▶ **Planning.** Planning is the process of determining how the work unit will contribute to organizational goals in the future. The manager's planning function includes developing processes and strategies.

- ▶ **Organizing.** The manager's organizational role is related to the tasks of preparing and allotting resources for the most efficient completion of tasks. Organizing involves setting up resources and systematizing processes to complete work requirements.

- ▶ **Directing.** As managers guide and supervise employees, they are engaging in the function of directing their work unit to contribute to organizational goals. The function of directing is likely to be related to the supervision processes that were discussed previously.

- ▶ **Controlling.** The function of controlling is important to maintaining the quality of work performed by a work unit. Outcomes are compared to the plan, and if they fall below expectations, the manager must identify shortcomings and implement improvements. Managerial functions can be seen as a cycle, beginning with the planning function and moving through organizing, directing, and controlling (Allen, 1998b). When needed, corrections are identified, and the planning stage is revisited so that strategies can be revised.

Managerial Roles

There are three major roles that managers must assume according to the demands of various situations (Allen, 1998c). Each role has subroles specific to the particular level of management. The primary roles are as follows:

- ▶ **Interpersonal role.** The manager must interact with numerous individuals and other organizations. In assuming the interpersonal role and depending on the situation, a manager may represent an organization in the community, his or her work unit to upper management, or upper management to the employees in his or her work unit.

- ▶ **Informational role.** The manager is responsible for collecting, monitoring, and disseminating information. The manager may receive and transmit information to and from a variety of sources, including outside the organization and both vertically and laterally within the organization.

▶ **Decisional role.** The decisional role requires the manager to determine how information is best used to meet organizational goals. The manager must make judgments regarding how information is to be disseminated and applied to goals, as well as how it will be used to meet changing demands and to allocate resources.

Managers assume multiple roles and exercise numerous skills.

▶ REFLECTION QUESTIONS

- How do management skills differ from leadership skills?
- Are there any similarities between or overlap of skills? Explain your answer.

8

LEADERSHIP SKILLS

Leaders are those who "challenge, inspire, enable, model, and encourage" (Kouzes & Posner, 1987, p. 1). Consider leadership as an attitude and a way of viewing events rather than as a position. Leadership skills are typically viewed as constructive and positive within an organization, and while it is beneficial for managers to possess leadership qualities, these characteristics can be developed by anyone to enhance his or her opportunities for career advancement. Consider developing the following attributes of a leader (Solomon, 2003).

▶ **Look to the future.** Leaders function in the present and attend to tasks at hand, yet at the same time are oriented to the future. A quality of leadership is being able to look ahead, see the future as a chance for growth and development, and communicate this vision to others.

▶ **View change as opportunity.** Leaders look for the positive elements of change. As part of looking to the future, leaders view change as a chance to make improvements.

▶ **Do your job ethically.** A quality of leadership is the ability to incorporate ethics into decisions and actions. Leaders demonstrate integrity by honoring regulatory guidelines and codes of ethics. Leaders strive for fairness and have a sense of justice.

▶ **Be oriented to people.** Leaders are aware of the needs of the people around them and honor their personal and professional needs, within reasonable limits. Leaders are able to direct, encourage, teach, mentor, or coach as the situation requires and do so in a manner that facilitates the development of those with whom they work.

▶ **Be open to learning.** Leaders make mistakes, and when they do, they approach mistakes as learning opportunities. Leaders admit to errors and strive to remedy them and to change their behavior based on what they have learned.

▶ **Think proactively.** Being proactive means looking ahead and anticipating needs. A leader communicates perceived future needs and supports efforts to respond to change constructively.

▶ **Take initiative.** Part of responding proactively is taking initiative. Taking initiative means being able to recognize a need and taking the responsibility to find a method of meeting it. At times, this may mean taking on responsibilities above and beyond those defined in one's job description. A leader sees what needs to be done and takes appropriate steps to initiate actions that are within ethical, professional, and legal boundaries. Taking initiative can be a significant factor in career advancement.

▶ **Be a problem solver.** Leaders do not see everything through "rose-colored glasses." Leaders approach issues with a problem-solving attitude by acknowledging problems and areas that, if improved, would contribute to a more effective organization. Far from being negative, leaders identify problems objectively, set emotional reactions aside, and offer feasible suggestions for improvement.

Comparison of Management and Leadership

Management Skills	Leadership Skills
Task oriented	People oriented
Concerned with the present	Concerned with building for the future
Practical	Visionary
More directive	More inspiring
Controls and manages others	Inspires and empowers others
Focuses on status quo	Focuses on innovation

FIGURE 8–1. Management skills and leadership skills are distinct, although they overlap in some ways. Most successful individuals possess both types of skills and apply each at appropriate times.

REFLECTION QUESTIONS

- What individual(s) have you perceived as a leader?
- What were the characteristics of the individual(s) that qualified him or her as a leader?

? CRITICAL THINKING QUESTIONS

8–2. Besides those mentioned, what other leadership characteristics can you identify?

8–3. How do leadership qualities contribute to an individual's professional advancement?

8–4. How do leaders and their attributes contribute to the growth of the organization?

REFLECTION QUESTIONS

- What strengths do you possess as a manager? Which management skills do you need to develop?
- What strengths do you possess as a leader? Which leadership skills do you need to develop?

---

success steps

TIPS FOR LEADERSHIP SKILL DEVELOPMENT

1. Look to the future.
2. View change as opportunity.
3. Do your job ethically.
4. Maintain an orientation to people.
5. Be open to learning.
6. Think proactively.
7. Take initiative.
8. Be a problem solver.

CHANGE MANAGEMENT

Change is inevitable in today's rapidly moving world. Thus, advancing your career depends significantly on your ability to respond to change (Pritchett, 1994). Consider the following suggestions for adjusting to change (Solomon & Jacobs, 2003):

▶ **Look for the opportunities in change.** Frequently, change opens new niches and creates advantages. A positive response to change involves identifying these opportunities and applying your skills and abilities to take advantage of them.

▶ **Recognize common emotional responses to change.** Individuals demonstrate a variety of responses to change, from strong resistance to excessive optimism. It is important to moderate responses to change by maintaining an objective outlook and approach. Leaders recognize their emotional responses and keep them in perspective, and help others do the same.

▶ **Be a creative problem solver.** Use creative thinking techniques to approach change and address the issues associated with it. Incorporate leadership skills by developing creative responses that reflect ethics and regulatory guidelines.

success steps

RESPONDING POSITIVELY TO CHANGE

1. Look for the opportunities in change.
2. Recognize common emotional responses to change.
3. Be a creative problem solver.

apply it

Management and Leadership

GOAL: To become familiar with the differences and similarities between management and leadership.

STEP 1: Conduct an Internet search for articles on management and leadership using "management" and "leadership" as your search terms. Consider having classmates complete the same search. Compare results and expand on each other's information as much as possible.

STEP 2: Write a compare-and-contrast paper exploring the similarities and differences between management and leadership. Ask any classmates who have completed the search activity to do the same.

STEP 3: Ask class members to present (anonymously, if they prefer) situations from their work experience that required supervisors' involvement. The situations should be presented in a manner that preserves the confidentiality of businesses and individuals. Review the scenarios as a class and discuss whether management or leadership techniques or a combination of both would have effectively addressed the situation.

STEP 4: Consider placing your research materials, your compare-and-contrast paper, and any insights you gain through this activity in your Learning Portfolio.

CHAPTER SUMMARY

Professional advancement depends on your ability to remain current and knowledgeable about developments in your field. This chapter outlined numerous sources for obtaining professional information and knowledge, including professional organizations, professional publications, electronic sources, and supervisors and mentors. Management and leadership skills were compared and were discussed in terms of how both can be developed to advance your career.

POINTS TO KEEP IN MIND

Several main points were discussed in detail in this chapter:

▶ Major factors in career advancement are being aware of current issues in your field, being able to apply new ideas to your work, and being able to adapt to change in your profession.

▶ Professional supervision involves numerous techniques, including teaching, directing, mentoring, and coaching.

▶ It is critical to keep records of your professional development, including documentation of continuing education for licensure and certification purposes.

▶ Your ability to continue learning contributes to your effectiveness in daily activities as well as to your career advancement in the form of promotions and the assumption of professional leadership roles.

▶ Professional development and continued learning are often linked with certifications and licenses that you must keep current in order to practice in your field.

▶ Taking advantage of the way in which you learn most effectively can greatly enhance your career advancement, because if you seek educational opportunities that are suited to your learning style, you will enjoy the process more and thus retain the information better.

▶ Professional organizations may be the most effective source of information for remaining current in your field.

▶ Professional organizations usually offer some form of annual conference and may sponsor seminars throughout the year.

▶ A professional organization's primary task is to serve the profession it represents and keep its membership informed. Consequently, up-to-date information from all areas of the profession is typically available.

▶ Most professional organizations produce a professional journal or other publication.

▶ In addition to the common search engines and other tools, the Internet provides opportunities for you to be automatically updated about a variety of subjects.

▶ Professional supervision is another tool for professional development.

▶ Interpersonal skills become increasingly critical with advancement to more senior levels of an organization, because management and leadership roles are typically more people oriented than strictly technical positions.

▶ Management skills relate to the mission and purpose of an organization and ensure that daily tasks are executed in a manner that contributes to organizational goals.

▶ Consider leadership as an attitude and a way of viewing events rather than as being a position.

▶ Developing leadership capabilities is possible regardless of your "official" position with your organization.

▶ Leadership skills include being oriented to the future; seeing the future as a chance for growth; being able to communicate that vision to others; and functioning with integrity, fairness, and a sense of justice.

▶ Taking initiative means anticipating people's needs and approaching mistakes with a problem-solving attitude.

▶ Advancing your career depends significantly on your ability to respond positively to change.

▶ A constructive approach to change include welcoming change as an opportunity for growth, understanding emotional responses to change, and approaching change with a spirit of creative problem-solving.

LEARNING OBJECTIVES REVISITED

Review the learning objectives for this chapter and rate your level of achievement for each objective using the rating scale provided. For each objective on which you do not rate yourself as a 3, outline a plan of action that you will take to fully achieve the objective. Include a time frame for this plan.

1 = did not successfully achieve objective

2 = understand what is needed, but need more study or practice

3 = achieved learning objective thoroughly

	1	2	3
Explain the importance of continued professional learning and development and its relationship to career advancement.	☐	☐	☐
Identify and locate resources for continued learning.	☐	☐	☐
Apply information about individual learning style to the professional development and career advancement strategies.	☐	☐	☐
Describe the professional supervision process and explain how supervision processes can be used to accomplish various professional development goals.	☐	☐	☐
Describe the skills, functions, and roles of management.	☐	☐	☐
Describe the skills of leadership.	☐	☐	☐
Compare and contrast management and leadership.	☐	☐	☐

Steps to Achieve Unmet Objectives

Steps	Due Date
1. _____	_____
2. _____	_____
3. _____	_____
4. _____	_____

8

SUGGESTED ITEMS FOR LEARNING PORTFOLIO

Refer to the "Developing Portfolios" section at the front of this textbook for more information on learning portfolios.

▶ Your Professional Organization: This activity is designed to familiarize you with your professional organization.

▶ Professional Listservs: The goal of this activity is to provide you with experience using a professional listserv.

▶ Identifying Your Learning Style: Complete this activity to understand how your learning style affects your professional development.

▶ Supervision Goals Management and Leadership: This activity will help you set supervision goals for your professional development.

▶ Communication Techniques: Complete this activity to develop your advanced communication skills.

▶ Management and Leadership: The goal of this activity is to familiarize you with management and leadership skills.

REFERENCES

Allen, G. (1998a). Management skills [electronic version]. Retrieved May 19, 2005, from http://ollie.dcccd.edu/mgmt1374/book_contents/1overview/management_skills/mgmt_skills.htm

Allen, G. (1998b). Managerial functions [electronic version]. Retrieved May 19, 2005, from http://ollie.dcccd.edu/mgmt1374/book_contents/1overview/managerial_functions/mgrl_functions.htm

Allen, G. (1998c). Managerial roles [electronic version]. Retrieved May 19, 2005, from http://ollie.dcccd.edu/mgmt1374/book_contents/1overview/managerial_roles/mgrl_roles.htm

Berger, S. (2003). Personnel considerations and supervision. In A. Solomon & K. Jacobs (Eds.), *Management Skills for the Occupational Therapy Assistant* (pp. 85–100). Thorofare, NJ: Slack, Inc.

Kouzes, J. M., & Posner, B. Z. (1987). *The Leadership Challenge.* San Francisco: Jossey-Bass.

Pritchett, P. (1994). *New Work Habits for a Radically Changing World: 13 Ground Rules for Job Success in the Information Age.* Dallas: Pritchett & Associates.

8

Solomon, A. (2003). The roles and responsibilities of the occupational therapy assistant in management. In A. Solomon & K. Jacobs (Eds.), *Management Skills for the Occupational Therapy Assistant* (pp. 1–21). Thorofare, NJ: Slack, Inc.

Solomon, A., & Jacobs, K. (2003). Change management. In A. Solomon & K. Jacobs (Eds.), *Management Skills for the Occupational Therapy Assistant* (pp. 23–28). Thorofare, NJ: Slack, Inc.

8

Conclusion

MOVING ON FROM HERE

You now have numerous concepts to apply toward successfully beginning your new career. You should come away from your experience with *100% Career Success* with ideas and strategies for presenting yourself and interacting as a confident and competent professional.

The most important part of learning is application. Remember to keep these concepts and ideas foremost in your mind so that you can readily apply them to your relationships and tasks in your new position. Use professional supervision and other resources to expand what you have learned in *100% Career Success* to develop your skills as a valuable employee and to develop career advancement strategies.

Again, congratulations on your educational achievements. May you have all the best as you pursue your career goals.

Index